SQL Server Interview Questions and Answers

For All Database Developers and Developers Administrators

Pinal Dave

SQLAuthority.com

Vinod Kumar

ExtremeExperts.com

Table of Contents

Email publisher@sqlauthority.com for bulk orders

Pinal Dave / Vinod Kumar
SQLAuthority.com / ExtremeExperts.com

Detailed Table of Contents

Pinal Dave / Vinod Kumar
SQLAuthority.com /ExtremeExperts.com

Pinal Dave / Vinod Kumar
SQLAuthority.com /ExtremeExperts.com

Pinal Dave / Vinod Kumar
SQLAuthority.com /ExtremeExperts.com

Pinal Dave / Vinod Kumar
SQLAuthority.com /ExtremeExperts.com

Pinal Dave / Vinod Kumar
SQLAuthority.com /ExtremeExperts.com

Pinal Dave / Vinod Kumar
SQLAuthority.com /ExtremeExperts.com

DATA WAREHOUSING INTERVIEW QUESTIONS & ANSWERS......................178

Pinal Dave / Vinod Kumar

Pinal Dave / Vinod Kumar
SQLAuthority.com /ExtremeExperts.com

About the Authors

Pinal Dave

Pinal works as a Technology Evangelist with Microsoft India. He has been a part of the IT industry for more than seven years. During his career he has worked both in India and the US, primarily with SQL Server Technology - right from version 6.5 to its latest form. Pinal has worked on many performance tuning and optimization projects for high transactional systems. He received his Master of Science from the University of Southern California and a Bachelors of Engineering from Gujarat University.

Additionally, he holds many Microsoft certificates. He has been a regular speaker at many international events like TechEd, SQL PASS, MSDN, TechNet, and countless user groups. Pinal writes frequently on his blog http://blog.SQLAuthority.com on various subjects concerning SQL Server technology and Business Intelligence. His passion for the community drives him to share his training and knowledge. Before joining Microsoft, he was awarded the Microsoft Most Valuable Professional (MVP) in SQL Server Technology for three continuous years for his outstanding community service. He was also awarded the Community Impact Award – Individual Contributor for 2010. When he is not in front of a computer, he is usually travelling to explore hidden treasures in nature with his toddler daughter, Shaivi, and his very supportive wife, Nupur.

Pinal is very active on social media – you can find him on twitter at http://twitter.com/pinaldave and on Facebook at http://facebook.com/SQLAuth

Pinal is also the co-author of two SQL Server books

- SQL Programming Joes 2 Pros: Programming & Development for Microsoft SQL Server 2008 (ISBN: 1451579489)
- SQL Wait Stats Joes 2 Pros: SQL server Performance Tuning Techniques Using Wait Types and Queues (ISBN: 1-4662-3477-6)

Vinod Kumar

Vinod Kumar has worked with SQL Server extensively since joining the industry over a decade ago. Working on various versions from SQL Server 7.0, Oracle 7.3 and other database technologies - he now works with Microsoft Technology Center (MTC) as a Technology Architect. With extensive database, BI and application background he currently helps customers maximize on the investments in technologies to solve real world business and integration problems. He has worked on various roles and projects involving development, migration, deployment, networking, architecture, testing, packaging, R&D for services and product based companies. He currently holds 26+ Microsoft Certifications on various technologies. Before joining Microsoft, he was a Microsoft MVP in SQL Server for more than 3 years.

In addition to his previous role inside Microsoft as Technology Evangelist (SQL Server), he is a known speaker at Technical conferences like Microsoft TechEd, MSDN, TechNet, GIDS. Vinod has more than 12+ years in computers and database systems since earning his Engineering degree from the College of Engineering, Guindy - Chennai. He has published numerous

Pinal Dave / Vinod Kumar
SQLAuthority.com /ExtremeExperts.com

articles in SQL Server on multiple sites and currently writes most of his learning over his site and blog at: http://blogs.ExtremeExperts.com. Feel free to follow on him on Twitter (@vinodk_sql).

Besides juggling all the activities, Vinod loves to watch movies, read books, explore food and enjoys spending time with his father (G.M.Sundaram) and supportive wife (Satya).

Acknowledgement

Rhonda Chesley is a SQL Server 2005 MCTS, an editor for Rick Morelan and all around geek wanna-be. She encourages girls of all ages to share her fascination of all things math and SQL.

Michael McLean has been working with Microsoft Technologies beginning in 1999 with Microsoft certifications in MCSE, MCSA, MCP+I, MCDBA and MCTS. Michael obtained his MCTS in Microsoft SQL 2008 Developer after attending Rick Morelan's school at MoreTechnology using the Joes2Pros books designed to help students pass Microsoft Exam 70-433 and now currently works at Microsoft in Redmond, WA on the Win7 Phone team.

Christopher Lennick earned a BS in Computer Science from Montana State University and has worked 26 years as an IT developer in various industries. He is currently employed by the largest natural and organic food distributor in the United States.

Preface

Today we are using computers for various activities, motor vehicles for traveling to places, and mobile phones for conversation. How many of us can claim the invention of micro-processor, a basic wheel, or the telegraph? Similarly, this book was not written overnight. The journey of this book goes many years back with many individuals to be thanked for.

To begin with, we want to thank all those interviewers who reject interviewees by saying they need to know 'the key things' regardless of having high grades in class. The whole concept of interview questions and answers revolves around knowing those 'key things'.

The core concept of this book will continue to evolve over time. I am sure many of you will come along with us on this journey and submit your suggestions to us to make this book a key reference for anybody who wants to start with SQL Server. Today we want to acknowledge the fact that you will help us keep this book alive forever with the latest updates. We want to thank everyone who participates in this journey with us.

Skills needed for this Book

We don't expect our readers to be experts in the workings of SQL Server, nor is this book geared towards a complete novice. If you have had some experience working with databases (especially SQL Server) this book can be a wonderful refresher for the fundamentals. The Question & Answers format is a quick reference for the common questions asked during an interview.

Pinal Dave / Vinod Kumar
SQLAuthority.com /ExtremeExperts.com

Feel free to use this as a cheat sheet prior to giving an interview and need a couple of questions to ask your candidate. If you are a student, please don't read this book and think it is a "sure to pass" reference to crack an interview. Instead, this book can be used to understand and get acquainted with some of the nuances and intricacies of SQL Server.

Having said all this, in God we trust and the rest we test. Feel free to test the concepts using actual code to reassert the concepts.

About this Book

As representatives of the IT community, we have certainly had our own experiences attending interviews where plenty of questions and doubts loomed...sometimes we failed miserably in the end! These stories have become pleasant (or not so pleasant) memories in our mind and this book will bring back some of those memories for sure. Once we analyzed the content of many, many interviews, we realized that most of them did not require a deep knowledge of the technical details of SQL, but they *did* require a solid understanding of the basics. Luckily, it is not necessary to know SQL inside and out to clear an interview. Subjects like "SQL Server" are so vast that it would take a lifetime to learn every detail of what it can do....even we learn something new every day!

There are a variety of careers for people who know SQL Server: Database Developer, Database Modelers, Database Architect, Database Administrator and many more. Hence, this book is geared towards demystifying and refreshing your memory of the fundamentals. Some of the concepts discussed are generic and are not tied to any specific version of SQL Server. That being said, most of the features are from SQL Server 2005 and 2008.

As we said before, this book is not a shortcut or a sure way to pass an interview. When faced with this big day, it is easy to get overwhelmed and not know where to begin. This guide will help you prepare in an organized manner. This book can be that secret sauce you use to prepare.

Now this book will flow in a "Question & Answer" mode from start to finish to help you grasp concepts faster and get to the point quickly. Once you understand the concepts, it gets easier to see twists using that concept within a scenario and to ultimately solve them. Most companies have an interview strategy specific to scenarios relevant to their environment, needs and SLAs (Service Level Agreements).

Though each of these chapters are geared towards convenience we highly recommend reading each of the sections irrespective of the roles you might be doing since each of the sections have some interesting trivia about working with SQL Server. In the industry the role of accidental DBA's (especially with SQL Server) is very common. Hence if you have performed the role of DBA for a short stint and want to brush-up your fundamentals then the upcoming sections will be a great review.

Education consists mainly of what we have unlearned. ~Mark Twain

Pinal Dave / Vinod Kumar
SQLAuthority.com /ExtremeExperts.com

Database Concepts with
SQL SERVER

Life consists not in holding good cards but in playing those you hold well
- Josh Billings.

What is RDBMS?

Relational Data Base Management Systems (RDBMS) are database management systems that maintain data records and indices in tables. Relationships may be created and maintained across and among the data and tables. In a relational database, relationships between data items are expressed by means of tables. Interdependencies among these tables are expressed by data values rather than by pointers. This allows a high degree of data independence. An RDBMS has the capability to recombine the data items from different files, providing powerful tools for data usage. (Read more here http://bit.ly/sqlinterview1)

What are the properties of the relational tables?

Relational tables have the following five properties:
- Values are atomic.
- Column values are of the same kind.
- The sequence of columns is insignificant.
- The sequence of rows is insignificant.
- Each column must have a unique name.

Pinal Dave / Vinod Kumar
SQLAuthority.com /ExtremeExperts.com

What is normalization?

Database normalization is a data design and organizational process applied to data structures based on rules that help build relational databases. In relational database design, the process of organizing data to minimize redundancy is called normalization. Normalization usually involves dividing database data into different tables and defining relationships between the tables. The objective is to isolate data so that additions, deletions, and modifications of a field can be made in just one table and then retrieved through the rest of the database via the defined relationships.

The key traits for Normalization are eliminating redundant data and ensuring data dependencies.

What is de-normalization?

De-normalization is the process of attempting to optimize the performance of a database by adding redundant data. It is sometimes necessary because current DBMSs implement the relational model poorly. A true relational DBMS would allow for a fully normalized database at the logical level, while providing physical storage of data that is tuned for high performance. De-normalization is a technique to move from higher to lower normal forms of database modeling in order to speed up database access.

De-normalizing the database design allows for fewer joins with tables and foreign key requirements. This method is commonly used for Reporting and OLAP workloads.

How is the ACID property related to databases?

ACID (an acronym for Atomicity Consistency Isolation Durability) is a concept that database professionals generally look for while evaluating relational databases and application architectures. For a reliable database, all four of these attributes should be achieved:

Atomicity is an all-or-none rule for database modifications.

Consistency guarantees that a transaction never leaves your database in a half-finished state.

Isolation keeps transactions separated from each other until they are finished.

Durability guarantees that the database will keep track of pending changes in such a way that the server can recover from an abnormal termination and committed transactions will not be lost. (Read more here http://bit.ly/sqlinterview3)

What are the different normalization forms?

1NF: Eliminate repeating groups

Make a separate table for each set of related attributes and give each table a primary key. Each field contains at most one value from its attribute domain.

Pinal Dave / Vinod Kumar
SQLAuthority.com /ExtremeExperts.com

2NF: Eliminate redundant data

If an attribute depends on only part of a multi-valued key, then remove it to a separate table.

3NF: Eliminate columns not dependent on the key

If attributes do not contribute to a description of the key, then remove them to a separate table. All attributes must be directly dependent on the primary key. (Read more here http://bit.ly/sqlinterview2)

BCNF: Boyce-Codd Normal Form

If there are non-trivial dependencies between candidate key attributes, then separate them out into distinct tables.

4NF: Isolate independent multiple relationships

No table may contain two or more 1:n or n:m relationships that are not directly related.

5NF: Isolate semantically related multiple relationships

There may be practical constraints on information that justifies separating logically related many-to-many relationships.

ONF: Optimal Normal Form

A model limited to only simple (elemental) facts, as expressed in Object Role Model notation.

Pinal Dave / Vinod Kumar
SQLAuthority.com /ExtremeExperts.com

DKNF: Domain-Key Normal Form

A model free from all modification anomalies are said to be in DKNF.

Remember, these normalization guidelines are cumulative. For a database to be in the 3NF, it must first fulfill all the criteria of a 2NF and 1NF database.

What is a stored procedure?

A stored procedure (SP) is a named group of SQL statements that have been created together and stored in the server database. Stored procedures are objects that do the work they are designed to do when you call upon them. You need to make sure they have what they need (the right values and parameters), so they can perform their important tasks. Stored procedures can act like views and select data, but they can also make updates, create objects, or even be set up to backup a database or perform other maintenance tasks.

Stored procedures accept input parameters so that a single procedure can be used over the network by several clients using different input data. When the procedure is modified, all clients automatically get the new version. Stored procedures reduce network traffic and improve performance. Stored procedures can be used to help ensure the integrity of the database logic. Typical system Stored Procedures are - sp_helpdb, sp_renamedb, sp_depends etc. (For a complete lesson on Stored Procedures see Chapters 6 and 7 of SQL Programming Joes 2 Pros Volume 4 ISBN: 1451579489)

Pinal Dave / Vinod Kumar

Execution plan retention, reuse and improved security from SQL injection are some of the advantages of using SPs. (Read more here http://bit.ly/sqlinterview4)

What is a Trigger?

A trigger is a SQL procedure or SQLCLR Code that initiates an action when an event (like INSERT, DELETE or UPDATE) occurs on an object. Based on events which take place in your database, you can have SQL Server "listen" for just the ones that should signal when it's time for actions to run automatically.

Triggers are stored in and managed by the DBMS. Triggers can be used to maintain the referential integrity of data by changing the data in a systematic fashion. A trigger cannot be called or executed directly; DBMS automatically fires the trigger as a result of a data modification to the associated table or in the case of DDL triggers to a DDL event in the database. Triggers are similar to stored procedures in that both consist of procedural logic that is stored at the database level. Stored procedures, however, are not event-driven and are not attached to a specific table as most triggers are. Stored procedures are explicitly executed by invoking a call to the procedure while triggers are implicitly executed by events. In addition, triggers can also execute stored procedures.

Nested trigger: A trigger can also contain INSERT, UPDATE and DELETE logic within itself; so when the trigger is fired because

Pinal Dave / Vinod Kumar
SQLAuthority.com /ExtremeExperts.com

of data modification, it can also cause data modification, thereby firing another trigger. A trigger is called a nested trigger when it is fired off from another trigger. (Read more here http://bit.ly/sqlinterview5)

SQL Server contains special triggers like logon triggers and DDL triggers.

What are the different types of triggers?

There are three types of triggers. (For a complete lesson on Triggers see Chapters 2 and 3 of SQL Programming Joes 2 Pros Volume 4 ISBN: 1451579489)

1) DML trigger

   There are two kinds of DML triggers

   a. Instead of Trigger
      Instead of Triggers are fired in place of the triggering action such as an insert, update, or delete.
   b. After Trigger
      After triggers execute following the triggering action, such as an insert, update, or delete.

2) DDL trigger
   This type of trigger is fired against DDL statements like Drop Table, Create Table, or Alter Table. DDL Triggers are always after Triggers.

Pinal Dave / Vinod Kumar
SQLAuthority.com /ExtremeExperts.com

> The data of DDL Triggers are captured in XML and called EventData which is available inside the trigger for logging at a later time.

3) Logon trigger

This type of trigger is fired against a LOGON event before a user session is established to the SQL Server.

What is a view?

A view can be thought of as a stored query accessible as a virtual table. It can be used for retrieving data as well as updating or deleting rows. Views in SQL Server provide a preset way to view data from one or more tables. They may also include aggregate fields (e.g., COUNT, SUM). Views allow your users to query a single object which behaves like a table and contains the needed joins and fields you have specified. In this way, a simple query (SELECT * FROM ViewName) can produce a more refined result which can serve as a report and answer business questions.

Rows updated or deleted in the view are updated or deleted in the table the view was created with. It should also be noted that as data in the original table changes, so does the data in the view-as views are the way to look at parts of the original table. The results of using a view are not permanently stored in the database. The data accessed through a view is actually constructed using a standard T-SQL select command and can come from one to many different base tables or even other views.

Pinal Dave / Vinod Kumar
SQLAuthority.com / ExtremeExperts.com

Two main purposes of creating a view are 1.) provide a security mechanism which restricts users to a certain subset of data and 2.) provide a mechanism for developers to customize how users can logically view the data.

What is an index?

An index is a physical structure containing pointers to the data. Indices are created in an existing table to locate rows more quickly and efficiently. It is possible to create an index on one or more columns of a table, and each index is given a name. During execution plan the users can see the index name but cannot see the indices themselves; they are just used to speed up queries. Effective indices are one of the best ways to improve performance of a database application.

An Index can give you improved query performance because a seek action occurs for retrieving records from your table in a query. A seek means you were able to locate record(s) without having to examine every row to locate those record(s).

A table scan occurs when there is no index available or when a poorly created index exists on the table for a query running against that table. In a table scan, SQL Server examines every row in the table to satisfy the query results. Table scans are sometimes unavoidable, but on large tables, scans have a significant impact on performance (For a complete lesson on Indices see Chapters 8-11 of SQL Architecture Basics Joes 2 Pros Volume 3 ISBN: 1451579462).

Maximum number of Indices from SQL Server 2008 is 1 clustered + 999 non-clustered indices. (Read more http://bit.ly/sqlinterview6)

What is a linked server?

A linked server configuration enables SQL Server to execute commands against OLE DB data sources on remote servers. With a linked server, you can create very clean, easy–to-follow SQL statements that allow remote data to be retrieved, joined, and combined with local data. The ability to issue distributed queries and perform commands with transactions on heterogeneous sources is one of the benefits of using linked servers.

The system supplied stored procedures sp_addlinkedserver and sp_addlinkedsrvlogin are used to add new linked server(s). The stored procedure sp_linkedservers is used to list all the linked servers defined on the server. (Read more here http://bit.ly/sqlinterview8)

What is a cursor?

A cursor is a database object used by applications in the procedural logic to manipulate data in a row-by-row basis, instead of the typical SQL commands that operate on all or parts of rows as sets of data.

In order to work with a cursor, we need to perform these steps in the following order:
- Declare a cursor
- Open the cursor

Pinal Dave / Vinod Kumar
SQLAuthority.com /ExtremeExperts.com

- Fetch a row from the cursor
- Process the fetched row
- Close cursor
- Deallocate the cursor (Read more here http://bit.ly/sqlinterview9)

What is a subquery? Explain the properties of a subquery?

Subqueries are often referred to as sub-selects as they allow a SELECT statement to be executed within the body of another SQL statement. A subquery is executed by enclosing it in a set of parentheses. Subqueries are generally used to return rows as an atomic value although they may be used to compare values against multiple rows with the IN keyword or they can return values in the case of correlated subqueries. There are two types of subqueries: basic subqueries and correlated subqueries. (For a complete lesson on subqueries see Chapters 11 of SQL Queries Joes 2 Pros Volume 2 ISBN: 1-4392-5318-8)

Some properties of basic subqueries:

- A basic subquery is a SELECT statement that is nested within another T-SQL statement.
- A basic subquery SELECT statement, if executed independently of the T-SQL statement in which it is nested, will return a result set. This implies that a subquery SELECT statement can stand alone, and it does not depend on the statement in which it is nested.

Pinal Dave / Vinod Kumar
SQLAuthority.com /ExtremeExperts.com

- A basic subquery SELECT statement can return any number of values and can be found in the column list of a SELECT statement, using FROM, GROUP BY, HAVING, and/or ORDER BY clauses of a T-SQL statement.
- A basic subquery can also be used as a parameter to a function call. Basically, a subquery can be used anywhere an expression can be used. (Read more here http://bit.ly/sqlinterview10)

What are Different Types of Joins?

Inner join

A join that displays only the rows that have a match in both joined tables is known as an inner Join. This is the default type of join in the query and also in View Designer.

Generally the INNER JOIN option is the most common join in application queries.

Outer joins

A join that includes rows even if they do not have related rows in the joined table is an outer join. You can create three different variations of an outer join to specify the unmatched rows to be included:

- **Left outer join:** In a left outer join, all the rows in the first-named table, i.e. "left" table, which appears leftmost in the JOIN clause, are included. An unmatched row in the right table appears as nulls in your result set.

- **Right outer join:** In a right outer join, all the rows in the second-named table, i.e. "right" table, which appears rightmost in the JOIN clause are included. An unmatched row in the left table will show nulls in your result set.

LEFT and RIGHT OUTER JOIN logic are opposite of each other. You can change either the order of the tables in the specific join statement or change the JOIN from left to right and get the same output.

- **Full outer join:** In a Full Outer Join, all of the rows all of the joined tables are included, whether they are matched or not.

Cross join

A cross join that does not have a WHERE clause produces the Cartesian product of the tables involved in the join. You can use a cross join to explore future possibilities. For example, at the beginning of a college semester, students may want to know what courses are required of them. Perhaps they have already satisfied some of those requirements. The requirements apply to all students regardless of the coursework they have done so far. A cross join simply returns all possible combinations of the record set data from the tables listed.

Pinal Dave / Vinod Kumar
SQLAuthority.com /ExtremeExperts.com

The size of a Cartesian product result set is *the number of rows in the first table multiplied by the number of rows in the second table.* One common example is when a company wants to combine each product with a pricing table to analyze each product at each price. (For a complete lesson on Cross Joins see Chapters 4 of Beginning SQL Joes 2 Pros Volume 1 ISBN: 1-4392-5317-X)

Self join

This is a special case when one table is joined to itself and aliasing the table name in one or two places to avoid confusion. A self join can be of any type (Inner Join or outer join), as long as the joined tables are the same. A self join is rather unique in that it involves a relationship with only one table. One common example is when a company has a hierarchal reporting structure wherein one member of the staff reports to another member of the staff. Self Joins are often used to show typical parts within other parts of the hierarchy. self joins can be an outer join or an inner join. (Read more here http://bit.ly/sqlinterview11)

Explain user-defined functions and their different variations?

A user-defined function takes zero or more input parameters and returns either a scalar value or a table. (For a complete lesson on Function see Chapter 8 of SQL Programming Joes 2 Pros Volume 4 ISBN: 1451579489)

Pinal Dave / Vinod Kumar
SQLAuthority.com /ExtremeExperts.com

The different types of user-defined functions created are as follows:

Scalar user-defined function

A scalar user-defined function returns one of the scalar data types (like Int, char, money, etc...). Text, ntext, image, timestamp, error handling, (XML data types are not supported).

These are the types of user-defined functions that developers can also use in other programming languages. (Read more here http://bit.ly/sqlinterview12)

Inline table-value user-defined function

An inline table-value user-defined function returns a table data type. This is an exceptional alternative to a view as the user-defined function can pass parameters into a T-SQL select command and in essence provide us with a parameterized, non-updateable view of the underlying tables.

Multi-statement table-value user-defined function

A multi-statement table-value user-defined function returns a table, and it is also an exceptional alternative to a view as the function can support multiple T-SQL statements to build the final result where the view is limited to a single SELECT statement. Also, the ability to pass parameters into a T-SQL select command or a group of them gives us the capability to create a parameterized, non-updateable view of the data in the underlying tables. Within the create function command, you must define the

Pinal Dave / Vinod Kumar

table structure that is being returned. After creating this type of user-defined function, it can be used in the FROM clause of a T-SQL command which is unlike using a stored procedure which can also return record sets. (Read more here http://bit.ly/sqlinterview13)

What is the difference between a user-defined function (UDF) and a stored procedure?

UDFs can be used in SQL statements anywhere in the WHERE/HAVING/SELECT section, whereas stored procedures cannot. UDFs that return tables can be treated as another rowset. This can be used in JOINs with other tables. Inline UDFs can be thought of as views that take parameters and can be used in JOINs and other rowset operations.

Stored procedures can be used with INSERT Statements. (Read more http://bit.ly/sqlinterview14)

What is an identity field?

An identity (or AutoNumber) is a column that automatically generates numeric values. An identity field uniquely differentiates (or identifies) each record in a table. In the case of an identity field, that distinct value is an identifying number (e.g., InvoiceID, ProductID). The noteworthy feature of identity fields is that the identity property enforces data integrity by automatically generating the ID value each time you add a new record to the table.

Pinal Dave / Vinod Kumar
SQLAuthority.com /ExtremeExperts.com

There can be only one IDENTITY column in a given table inside SQL Server. A starting value and an increment value can be set, but most DBAs choose to start at 1. A GUID (Global Unique Identifier) column also generates numbers; the value of the identity cannot be controlled.

TRUNCATE TABLE resets the IDENTITY column to its base value. The DELETE command doesn't do this.

What is the correct order of the Logical Query Processing Phases?

People often think that in a typical SELECT * FROM type of query the SELECT runs first since it is always on top. Actually, when the query executes it runs the FROM clause first. The correct order of the Logical Query Processing Phases are as follows:

1. FROM
2. ON
3. OUTER
4. WHERE
5. GROUP BY
6. CUBE | ROLLUP
7. HAVING
8. SELECT
9. DISTINCT
10. ORDER BY
11. TOP

(Read more here http://bit.ly/sqlinterview15)

Pinal Dave / Vinod Kumar
SQLAuthority.com /ExtremeExperts.com

What is a PRIMARY KEY?

A PRIMARY KEY constraint is a unique identifier for a row within a database table. A primary key prevents, duplicates, and ensures that all records have their own distinct values. Primary keys don't allow nulls, so you are guaranteed that each record has its own unique populated value.

Every table should have a primary key constraint to uniquely identify each row, and only one primary key constraint can be created for each table. The primary key constraints are used to enforce entity integrity. (For a complete lesson on all types of keys and constraints see Chapter 1 of SQL Programming Joes 2 Pros Volume 4 ISBN: 1451579489)

It is not possible to change the length of a column defined with a PRIMARY KEY constraint. If you need to change the length then you must first delete the existing PRIMARY KEY constraint and then re-create it with the new definition.

What is a FOREIGN KEY?

A FOREIGN KEY constraint prevents any actions that would destroy links between tables with the corresponding data keys. A simple way to think of a foreign key is that, essentially, it is another field which has a corresponding primary key field.

A foreign key in one table points to a primary key or unique key on another table. Foreign keys prevent actions that would change rows with foreign key values when there are no primary keys with that value. The foreign key constraints are used to enforce referential integrity.

What is a UNIQUE KEY Constraint?

A UNIQUE constraint enforces the uniqueness of the values in a set of columns; so no duplicate values are entered. The unique key constraints are used to enforce entity integrity as the primary key constraints.

Primary key is also a unique key internally, but cannot allow NULLs. unique keys on the other hand allow a single NULL but not multiple NULLs over the columns. (Read more here http://bit.ly/sqlinterview16)

What is a CHECK constraint?

A CHECK constraint is used to limit the values that can be placed in a column. CHECK constraints are most often used to enforce domain integrity. (Read more here http://bit.ly/sqlinterview17)

What is a NOT NULL constraint?

A not null constraint enforces that the column will not accept null values. Not null constraints are used to enforce domain integrity.
(Read more here http://bit.ly/sqlinterview18)

What is a DEFAULT definition?

A DEFAULT definition is used to add values into a column when values were omitted. The default value must be compatible with the data type of the column to which the DEFAULT definition applies. (For a complete lesson on Default Constraints see Chapter 1 of SQL Programming Joes 2 Pros Volume 4 ISBN: 1451579489)

Pinal Dave / Vinod Kumar
SQLAuthority.com /ExtremeExperts.com

DEFAULT values can be in integer and datetime fields but cannot be defined on timestamp and IDENTITY columns.

What are catalog views?

Catalog views return information that is used by the SQL Server database engine. Catalog views are the most general interface to the catalog metadata and provide the most efficient way to obtain, transform, and present customized forms of this information. All user-available catalog metadata is exposed through catalog views.

Points to Ponder from Beginning SQL Joes 2 Pros Volume 1 (ISBN: 1-4392-5317-X) (Joes2Pros.com)

1. A query is written in the SQL language and is a request for information from data in a database.

2. Microsoft SQL Server uses the Transact Structured Query Language (T-SQL).

3. The percent % symbol is the most common wildcard. This symbol represents any number of characters. For example, **WHERE Firstname like '%N'** would find a name that ends in N regardless of how long the name is. Examples may include Ann, MaryAnn and Dean among others.

4. The % sign can even represent zero characters. For example, **'%A%'** would find Alex and Lisa.

5. The SQL operator LIKE can be used to return a range of names, such as those beginning with a letter ranging from A to M. For example, **WHERE Firstname LIKE '[a-m]%'**

Pinal Dave / Vinod Kumar
SQLAuthority.com /ExtremeExperts.com

6. If you want to "exact match" a % symbol, like the name R%per!est and all other names with a percent symbol in them, surround the wildcard with square brackets. For example, **LastName LIKE '%[%]%'**

7. An inner join only returns a result set with perfectly matched values from fields in two or more tables.

8. An inner join is the default join type. If inner is omitted from the join clause of a query, SQL Server will assume it to be an inner join.

9. In a left outer join, the table named before the join might have records that appear even if SQL Server finds no matching records in the table listed after the LEFT OUTER JOIN clause.

10. The table listed after the RIGHT OUTER JOIN might have records that appear even if no matching records are found in the table on the left of the join.

11. When you alias a table, you use an abbreviation. SQL aliasing usually means using a shorter name than the original identifier.

12. A cross join creates or finds all possible entity combinations. The cross join does not need to use an ON clause.

13. Column names for a table must be unique. You can't have two fields named Hiredate in the same table.

14. A CREATE TABLE statement is a DDL statement. DDL means Data Definition Language. CREATE and DROP are DDL keywords.

15. Data Definition Language (DDL) statements handle the structure or design of database objects (e.g., databases

Pinal Dave / Vinod Kumar
SQLAuthority.com /ExtremeExperts.com

and tables) whereas Data Manipulation Language (DML) statements affect the actual data content. SELECT, INSERT, UPDATE and DELETE are four key DML keywords

16. Before SQL 2008 you could only insert 1 record with one insert statement. New to SQL 2008 is a feature called Row Constructors where you can insert many records at once with one insert statement.

17. SQLCMD is a command-line utility that allows you to run sql scripts or Ad-Hoc SQL queries.

18. BCP stands for Bulk Copy Program. BCP lets you perform data imports and exports using a command-line utility.

19. A transaction is a group of SQL statements treated as a single unit. Transactions ensure data integrity.

20. Transaction statements either all execute together or they don't at all.

21. If one statement can't run then the transaction is not committed.

22. A failed statement in a transaction means all data in the intermediate state gets discarded and none of the records will be committed.

23. The BEGIN TRANSACTION statement marks the beginning of a group of SQL statements in a transaction.

24. The COMMIT TRANSACTION marks the end of the transaction and saves all the changes to SQL's permanent storage.

25. If you want to read dirty data, you can use the READUNCOMMITTED table hint in your query.

26. The NOLOCK and READUNCOMMITTED table hints operate identically. Since NOLOCK is easier to type, it is used more often.

27. The advantage to the NOLOCK or READUNCOMMITTED table hints is your query runs without waiting for another process to release its locks.

28. To log into SQL Server, you need to create a server-level login. There are two types of server level logins (SQL Logins, Windows Logins).

29. Permissions can be manipulated with these DCL statements: GRANT, DENY, and REVOKE.

30. If you DENY a permission, it trumps any other permissions to that object or scope. For example, if you grant control and deny control, the user would have no access to the securable.

31. To remove an existing granted or denied permission, use the REVOKE keyword.

Common Generic Questions & Answers

Don't think outside the box. Think like there is no B O X. - unknown

What is OLTP (Online Transaction Processing)?

In OLTP (Online Transaction Processing systems), relational database design uses the discipline of data modeling and generally follows the Codd rules of data normalization in order to ensure absolute data integrity. Using these rules, complex information is broken down into its most simple structure (a table) where all of the individual atomic level elements relate to each other and satisfy the normalization rules.

What are pessimistic and optimistic locks?

Optimistic locking is a strategy where you read a record, take note of a version number and check that the version hasn't changed before you write the record back. If the record is changed (i.e. a different version to yours), then you abort the transaction and the user can re-start the transaction with the new data and update appropriately.

Pessimistic locking is when you lock the record for your exclusive use until you have finished with it. There are 4 levels of locking in the pessimistic isolation levels from lowest to highest. They are: read uncommitted, read committed, repeatable read, and serializable. At the serializable level (the highest locking and isolation level) it has much better integrity than optimistic locking but requires you to be careful with your application design to avoid deadlocks.

What are the different types of locks?

- **Shared locks:** Used for operations that do not change or update data (read-only operations), such as a SELECT statement.
- **Update locks:** Used on resources that can be updated. It prevents a common form of deadlock that occurs when multiple sessions are reading, locking, and potentially updating resources later.
- **Exclusive locks:** Used for data-modification operations, such as INSERT, UPDATE, or DELETE. It ensures that multiple updates cannot be made to the same resource at the same time.
- **Intent locks:** Used to establish a lock hierarchy. The types of intent locks are: intent shared (IS), intent exclusive (IX), and shared with intent exclusive (SIX).
- **Schema locks:** Used when an operation dependent on the schema of a table is executed. The types of schema locks are schema modification (Sch-M), and schema stability (Sch-S).
- **Bulk Update Locks:** Used when bulk-copying data into a table and the TABLOCK hint is specified.

What is the difference between an update lock and exclusive lock?

When exclusive lock is on any process, no other lock can be placed on that row or table. Every other process has to wait until the exclusive lock completes its tasks.

An update lock is a type of exclusive lock, except that it can be placed on the row which already has shared lock on it. Update lock reads the data of the row which has the shared lock. As soon as the update lock is ready to change the data it converts itself to the exclusive lock. (Read more here http://bit.ly/sqlinterview19)

What is new in lock escalation in SQL Server 2008?

Lock escalation is one of the lesser known phenomena inside SQL Server. Often times locking 1 row in a table cost less than locking the entire table. If you are updating thousands of records at once then SQL might find that is less costly to lock the table once rather than locking thousands of individual rows.

SQL Server uses this to minimize the overhead of locking too many structures by escalating the locks from just row locks to page locks to table locks. There is now a lock escalation option in the alter table of SQL Server 2008 which allows the disabling of lock escalation on that table.

What is the NOLOCK hint?

Using the NOLOCK query optimizer hint is generally considered a good practice in order to improve concurrency on a busy system especially for Reporting workloads. When the NOLOCK hint is included in a SELECT statement, no locks are taken when data is read. The result can be a dirty read, which means that another process already started updating the data before you read it. There are no guarantees that your query will retrieve the most recent data.

The advantage to performance is that your reading of data will not block updates from taking place, and updates will not block your reading of data. SELECT statements generally take shared (read) locks which are avoided because of this hint. With this shared (read) lock in place (when you don't use NOLOCK) multiple SELECT statements are allowed simultaneous access, but other processes are blocked from modifying the data. (To read more on this topic go here: http://bit.ly/sqlinterview20)

What is the difference between the DELETE and TRUNCATE commands?

The delete command removes the rows from a table on the basis of the condition that we provide a WHERE clause. Truncate will actually remove all of the rows from a table, and there will be no data in the table after we run the truncate command. (For a complete lesson on TRUNCATE and DELETE see Chapter 12 of SQL Queries Joes 2 Pros Volume 2 ISBN: 1-4392-5318-8)

TRUNCATE

- TRUNCATE is faster and uses fewer system and transaction log resources than DELETE.
- TRUNCATE removes the data by deallocating the data pages used to store the table's data, and only the page deallocations are recorded in the transaction log.
- TRUNCATE removes all the rows from a table, but the table structure, its columns, constraints, indexes, and permissions remain. You cannot use TRUNCATE TABLE on a table referenced by a FOREIGN KEY constraint. As TRUNCATE TABLE is not logged, it cannot activate a trigger.
- TRUNCATE cannot be rolled back unless it is used in a TRANSACTION. (To read more on this topic go here: http://bit.ly/sqlinterview127)
- TRUNCATE is a DDL Command.
- TRUNCATE resets the identity field of the table

DELETE

- DELETE removes one record at a time If used with a predicate in a where clause and records an entry in the transaction log for each deleted row.
- If you want to retain the identity counter, use DELETE instead. If you want to remove table definition and its data, use the DROP TABLE statement.
- DELETE can be used with or without a WHERE clause
- DELETE activates triggers.

Pinal Dave / Vinod Kumar
SQLAuthority.com /ExtremeExperts.com

- DELETE can be rolled back.
- DELETE is a DML Command.
- DELETE does not reset the identity of the table.
  (Read more here http://bit.ly/sqlinterview21)

What is connection pooling and why is it used?

To minimize the cost of opening and closing connections, ADO.NET uses an optimization technique called connection pooling. The pooler maintains ownership of the physical connection. It manages connections by keeping alive a set of active connections for each given connection configuration. Whenever a user creates an open connection, the pooler looks for an available connection in the pool. If a pooled connection is available, it returns it to the caller instead of opening a new connection. When the connection is closed, the pooler returns it to the pooled set of active connections instead of closing it. Once the connection is returned to the pool, it is ready to be reused on the next open connection.

Only connections with the same configuration can be pooled. ADO.NET keeps several pools at the same time, one for each configuration.

What is collation?

Collation refers to a set of rules that determines how data is sorted and compared. Character data is sorted using rules that define the correct character sequence with options for specifying case sensitivity, accent marks, Kana character types,

Pinal Dave / Vinod Kumar
SQLAuthority.com /ExtremeExperts.com

and character width. (Read more here http://bit.ly/sqlinterview23)

> After a collation has been assigned to any object or database, you cannot change the collation unless you drop and re-create the object/database.

What are different types of collation sensitivity?

Case sensitivity - A and a, B and b, etc.

*Accent sensitiv*ity - a and á, o and ó, etc.

Kana Sensitivity - When Japanese Kana, Hiragana, and Katakana characters are treated differently, it is called Kana sensitive.

Width sensitivity – When a single-byte character (half-width) and the same character represented as a double-byte character (full-width) are treated differently, it is width sensitive. (Read more here http://bit.ly/sqlinterview24)

How do you check collation and compatibility level for a database?

The following query can be used to see the collation and compatibility level your databases:

```
SELECT compatibility_level,
collation_name
FROM sys.databases
WHERE name ='YOUR DATABASE NAME HERE'
```

What is a dirty read?

A dirty read occurs when two operations, say, READ and WRITE occur together giving the incorrect or intermediate data. Suppose, User1 changed a row but did not commit the changes and User2 then reads the uncommitted data. The data may be wrong if User 2 does a rollback because the intermediate data may never have been committed. Because data in the intermediate state may never have been committed, it is considered a dirty read.

What is snapshot isolation?

Snapshot isolation is one type of pessimistic locking concurrency. SQL Server 2005 introduced this new snapshot isolation level to enhance concurrency for OLTP applications. Once snapshot isolation is enabled, updated row versions for each transaction are maintained in the tempdb. : So any transaction that requests a record that is in-between transactions will make the last consistent committed value visible to the user. (to read more on this topic go here: http://bit.ly/sqlinterview25)

SQL Server extends the SQL-92 isolation levels with the introduction of the SNAPSHOT isolation.

What is the difference between a HAVING clause and a WHERE clause?

The HAVING clause specifies a search condition for a GROUP BY or an aggregate. The difference is that HAVING can be used only with the SELECT statement whereas the WHERE can be

Pinal Dave / Vinod Kumar
SQLAuthority.com /ExtremeExperts.com

used during update and delete operations. HAVING is typically used with a GROUP BY clause. The HAVING clause is used in an aggregate function or a GROUP BY clause in a query, whereas a WHERE Clause is applied to each row before they are part of the GROUP BY clause or aggregate function in a query. (Read more here http://bit.ly/sqlinterview26)

What is a B-tree?

The database server uses a B-tree structure to organize index information. B-tree generally has the following types of index pages or nodes:

- *Root node:* A root node contains node pointers to only one branch node.
- *Branch nodes:* A branch node contains pointers to two or more leaf nodes or other branch nodes.
- *Leaf nodes:* A leaf node contains index items and horizontal pointers to two or more leaf nodes.

What are the different index configurations a table can have?

A table can have one of the following index configurations.
- No indexes
- A clustered index only
- A clustered index with one non-clustered indexes
- A non-clustered index with no clustered index
- A clustered index with many non-clustered indices
- Many non-clustered indices with no clustered index

Pinal Dave / Vinod Kumar
SQLAuthority.com /ExtremeExperts.com

What is a filtered index?

A filtered index is used to index a portion of the rows in a table. This means it applies a filter on an INDEX which improves query performance, reduces index maintenance costs, and reduces index storage costs when compared with full-table indices. When we see an index created with a WHERE clause, then that is actually a Filtered Index. (Read more here http://bit.ly/sqlinterview27)

What are indexed views inside SQL Server?

Views are a description of the data (aka metadata). When a view is referenced in the FROM clause its metadata is retrieved from a system catalog and placed into a query. While working with a non-indexed view, the portion of the view is resolved at run time. These are a departure from "regular" views, because placing an index on a view causes the view to be materialized persistently – that is, not just at runtime – and it retains a copy of the data

In case of an indexed view the view's result set is materialized immediately and persists in physical storage in the database. During run time this materialized storage is used to resolve the query result. An Indexed View is primarily created when expecting performance improvement from the query that uses that index.

What are some of the restrictions of indexed views?

There are plenty of restrictions for indexed views. If an Index is created on a view, then the definition of the view **must not** contain any of the following:

Pinal Dave / Vinod Kumar
SQLAuthority.com /ExtremeExperts.com

- ANY, NOT ANY
- OPENROWSET, OPENQUERY, OPENDATASOURCE
- arithmetic on imprecise (float, real) values
- OPENXML
- COMPUTE, COMPUTE BY
- ORDER BY (Read more here http://bit.ly/sqlinterview28)
- CONVERT producing an imprecise result
- OUTER join (Read more here http://bit.ly/sqlinterview29)
- COUNT(*) (Read more here http://bit.ly/sqlinterview30)
- reference to a base table with a disabled clustered index
- GROUP BY ALL
- reference to a table or function in a different database (Read more here http://bit.ly/sqlinterview31)
- Derived table (subquery in FROM list)
- reference to another view (Read more here http://bit.ly/sqlinterview32)
- DISTINCT
- ROWSET function
- EXISTS, NOT EXISTS
- self-join (Read more here http://bit.ly/sqlinterview33)
- expressions on aggregate results (e.g. SUM(x)+SUM(x))
- STDEV, STDEVP, VAR, VARP, AVG
- full-text predicates (CONTAINS, FREETEXT, CONTAINSTABLE, FREETEXTTABLE)
- A Subquery

- imprecise constants (e.g. 2.34e5)
- SUM on nullable expressions
- inline or table-valued functions
- table hints (e.g. NOLOCK)
- MIN, MAX
- text, ntext, image, filestream, or XML columns
- non-deterministic expressions
- TOP
- non-unicode collations
- UNION (Read more here http://bit.ly/sqlinterview34)
- Contradictions predicates making the view empty would be can be detected in SQL Server 2005 and newer (e.g. where 0=1 and ...)

Indexed views sometimes have very interesting behavior which can negate the whole purpose of the Indexed Views. (Read more here http://bit.ly/sqlinterview35)

What are DMVs and DMFs used for?

The DMVs (Dynamic Management Views) and DMFs (Dynamic Management Functions) were introduced in SQL Server 2005. It gives the database administrator information about the current state of the SQL Server machine on various aspects. From the basic definition, these dynamic management views and functions replace many of the DBCC command outputs and the pseudo table outputs. Hence, it is far easier to detect the health of SQL Server using these views and functions.

Pinal Dave / Vinod Kumar
SQLAuthority.com /ExtremeExperts.com

What are statistics inside SQL Server?

Statistics are the heart and soul of the SQL Server engine. SQL Server looks at the data in its tables long before you run your first SELECT statement. Because it's already done this, SQL Server knows how best to run a query when the time comes. Sampling of this data is stored in statistics, so the query optimizer can make the right decisions.

Without Statistics, the SQL Server Engine's Query Optimizer cannot decide the most optimal execution plan for the query. Statistics are used for SELECT, INSERT, UPDATE and DELETE operations. It is very important to keep statistics updated for SQL server to use the most efficient low resource execution plan. You can check the statistics on any table using the following command.

```
USE AdventureWorks
GO
sp_helpstats 'Person.Contact';
```

For a complete lesson on Statistics see Chapters 12 of SQL Architecture Basics Joes 2 Pros Volume 3 ISBN: 1451579462.

Points to Ponder from SQL Queries Joes 2 Pros Volume 2 ISBN: 1-4392-5318-8 (Joes2Pros.com)

1. The ORDER BY clause enables you to sort your query results. You can append the DESC (descending) and ASC (ascending) keywords to your ORDER BY clause.

2. If null values appear in your sort, they are first in ASC queries and last in DESC queries.

Pinal Dave / Vinod Kumar
SQLAuthority.com /ExtremeExperts.com

3. In SQL Server 7.0 and newer you can join up to 256 tables in a single query.

4. Databases often contain tables which exist for the sole purpose of allowing indirect relationships for Many-to-Many relationships between tables. These intermediary tables are known as Mapping Tables, Bridge Tables, or Junction Tables.

5. When filtering for nulls in queries, use the IS NULL or IS NOT NULL operators.

6. You can create expression fields in your query and base them upon other fields (like having a foreign currency price based upon the US price). An expression field is sometimes called a calculated field, a dynamic field, or a derived field.

7. The ANSI equivalent of GETDATE( ) is the property CURRENT_TIMESTAMP.

8. When using an aggregated function in your select list like Sum or Count you must have supporting aggregated language like GROUP BY or OVER.

9. The HAVING clause always appears after the GROUP BY clause. HAVING sets conditions on the aggregated values of the GROUP BY clause similar to the way WHERE interacts with SELECT.

10. The DISTINCT clause is useful to show all items in your query once, regardless of how many times they are listed. Use DISTINCT to eliminate duplicates or multiple listings of the same entity value when they are not relevant to your report. You can combine DISTINCT and HAVING to find aggregates that don't count repeating records multiple times.

Pinal Dave / Vinod Kumar
SQLAuthority.com /ExtremeExperts.com

11. A differing record count using a SELECT query vs. SELECT DISTINCT can be a rapid way to know if duplication exists.

12. With the OVER( ) clause you can integrate both actual base fields and aggregates in the same row. OVER( ) allows aggregation without requiring you to use a GROUP BY clause.

13. The OVER clause can aggregate rows across groups of another field using the PARTITON BY keyword. For example a grocery chain can find how sales of bananas compare to total produce sales instead of the entire food total sales. Leaving the OVER( ) blank causes it to apply the aggregation across all rows of the query.

14. The TOP results you see are based on your sorting order. For example, if you sort by SALES DESC you would see the largest sales at the top of the record set. If you choose SALES ASC, then the lowest sales would be listed at the top of the result set.

15. TOP is strictly a row limiter and does not evaluate or "read" data values. (It relies upon your sort order and slices off the specified number of records from the upper part of the result set.) When you add the keyword WITH TIES, it evaluates the data to include any tying values.

16. SQL Server has four ranking functions: RANK( ), DENSE_RANK( ), ROW_NUMBER( ), and NTILE( ).

17. DENSE_RANK( ) counts ties and uses sequential number sequencing (no skipping, no gaps). Dense ranking closes the number gap caused by multiple rows having the same rank number. RANK( ) assigns tie records the same rank (three records tied for 6th place will all receive the rank of 6). After the tie is broken, RANK( ) assigns the next

Pinal Dave / Vinod Kumar

record's row position as the rank (after the three records tied for 6th place, RANK( ) will assign 9 as the rank of the next record).

18. The ROW_NUMBER( ) function is very similar to the RANK() and DENSE_RANK() functions. Use the ROW_NUMBER( ) function to number rows with no ties and no skipping.

19. Like ROW_NUMBER, the NTILE( ) function ignores values, including ties. All records are handled in order and assigned to their respective groups. Records with the same value can be placed into separate groups. NTILE distributes rows into a specified number of groups.

20. When using the UNION or UNION ALL operators you get record sets that are combined from multiple sources.

21. UNION or UNION ALL operators require that all listed queries have the same number and type of fields in the same order.

22. Since all the fields in the UNION have compatible (if not identical) data types, then it does not matter if the column names match. For example, you can union CustomerID and ProductID since both of these fields are the same data type (integer).

23. In a UNION query only distinct records are selected. No duplicates.

24. Using UNION ALL returns all records, including duplicates.

25. Because UNION checks record by record to filter out duplicates, its processing time will be longer than a UNION ALL, which does not check for duplicates.

Pinal Dave / Vinod Kumar
SQLAuthority.com /ExtremeExperts.com

Common Developer Questions

The tragedy of life doesn't lie in not reaching your goal. The tragedy lies in having no goals to reach. - Benjamin Mays

What is blocking?

SQL Server blocking occurs when one connection places a lock on a table (or selected rows, pages, extent) and another connection attempts to read or modify the data when the lock is in effect. Another connection has to wait until the resources are released from the original connection which is holding the lock on the resources. Blocking often happens on the server when the system is under heavy transactional workload on a single resource. The way to resolve blocking is to identify the blocking statements which will then allow optimization of the blocking statements (re-write T-SQL, Indexing, or other configuration changes).

What is a deadlock? How can you identify and resolve a deadlock?

Deadlocking occurs when two user processes have locks on separate objects and each process is trying to acquire a lock on the object that the other process has locked. When a deadlock happens SQL server will then select the process with the least amount of overhead to rollback or abort. This way a deadlock is automatically resolved. There are multiple ways to

SQLAuthority.com Pinal Dave / Vinod Kumar
/ExtremeExperts.com

identify deadlocks i.e. Profile Deadlock Graph, DMV - sys.dm_tran_locks, and Extended Events.

How is a deadlock different from a blocking situation?

A deadlock occurs when two or more tasks permanently block each other by having a lock on a resource which the other task is trying to lock. In a deadlock situation, both transactions in the deadlock will wait forever unless the deadlock is broken. While in a standard blocking scenario, the blocked task will simply wait until the blocking task releases the conflicting lock.

Deadlocks can occur on resources other than database objects.

What is the maximum row size for a table?

The maximum bytes per row is 8086 (MSDN - http://bit.ly/sqlinterview131) in SQL Server 2008 R2. Additionally maximum bytes per varchar(max), varbinary(max), xml, text, or image column is 2GB (2^31-1). For a complete lesson on Date Types and Row Usage see Chapter 3 of SQL Architecture Basics Joes 2 Pros Volume 3 ISBN: 1451579462

SQL Server 2005 and later versions can handle more than 8086 bytes of data by moving the record to another page in the ROW_OVERFLOW_DATA allocation unit. In the original page it maintains a 24-byte pointer to this ROW_OVERFLOW_DATA allocation unit. (Read more here http://bit.ly/sqlinterview36).

What are sparse columns?

The sparse data option is a new SQL Server 2008 feature for fields you expect to be predominantly null. Using the sparse data option, you can instruct SQL Server to not have nulls consume space in sparsely populated fields. For a complete lesson on Sparse see Chapter 4 of SQL Architecture Basics Joes 2 Pros Volume 3 ISBN: 1451579462

Occasionally you will encounter a column in your database which is rarely used. For example, suppose you have a field called Violation in an Employee table but very few employees have any violations – perhaps two or three for every 1000 employees. In this case, over 99% of the Violation field values are null. This would be a sparsely populated field.

A sparse column is another tool used to reduce the amount of physical storage used in a database. They are ordinary columns that are optimized for the storage of null values. Sparse columns reduce the space requirements for null values at the cost of more overhead to retrieve non-null values. (Read more here http://bit.ly/sqlinterview37)

What are XML column-sets with SPARSE columns?

Tables that use sparse columns can designate a column to return all sparse columns in the table to XML data. A column set is like a calculated column in that the column set is not physically stored in the table. A column set differs from a calculated column in that the column set is directly updatable.

What is the maximum number of columns a table can have?

Maximum columns per table is 1024 in SQL Server 2008 R2.

A wide table is a table with a column set. This mean it contains SPARSE column(s), in this case the columns per table limit is 30,000. (MSDN - http://bit.ly/sqlinterview132)

What are INCLUDED columns with SQL Server indices?

In SQL Server 2005 and later versions, the functionality of non-clustered indices is extended by adding non-key columns to the leaf level of the non-clustered index. Non-key columns can help to create covered indices. By including non-key columns, you can create non-clustered indices that cover more queries. The database engine does not consider non-key columns when calculating the number of index key columns or index key size. For a complete lesson on included columns in an index see Chapter 9 of SQL Architecture Basics Joes 2 Pros Volume 3 ISBN: 1451579462

Non-key columns can be included in non-clustered indices to avoid exceeding the current index size limitations of a maximum of 16 key columns and a maximum index key size of 900 bytes. Another advantage is that using a non-key column in an index we can have index data types not allowed as index key columns generally. (To read more on this topic go here: http://bit.ly/sqlinterview38)

Pinal Dave / Vinod Kumar
SQLAuthority.com /ExtremeExperts.com

What are INTERSECT operators?

The four multi-query operators are UNION, UNION ALL INTERSECT, and EXCEPT. The INTERSECT operator introduced in SQL Server 2005 and later versions is used to retrieve the common records from both the left and the right query of the INTERCECT operator. The INTERSECT operator returns almost the same results as an INNER JOIN clause for all of the fields listed in the query. When using the INTERSECT operator the number and the order of the columns must be the same in all queries and the data type must be compatible. (Read more here http://bit.ly/sqlinterview39)

What is the EXCEPT Operator use for?

The EXCEPT operator is similar to the MINUS operation in Oracle. The EXCEPT query and MINUS query return all rows in the first query that are not found in the second query. For a complete lesson on Multiple Query Operators Chapters 8 of SQL Queries Joes 2 Pros Volume 2 ISBN: 1-4392-5318-8

Each SQL statement within the EXCEPT query (and MINUS query in Oracle) must have the same number of fields in the result sets with similar data types. (Read more here http://bit.ly/sqlinterview40)

What are GROUPING SETS?

The GROUPING SETS, ROLLUP, and CUBE operators are added to the GROUP BY clause. Though the results can be mimicked by using UNION ALL operators, these new constructs are far more efficient. There is a new function, GROUPING_ID(), that returns more grouping-level information than the existing

GROUPING() function. The non-ISO compliant WITH ROLLUP, WITH CUBE, and ALL syntax is being deprecated.

The new ROLLUP and CUBE syntax is only available in compatibility level 100.

What are row constructors inside SQL Server?

Transact-SQL is enhanced to allow multiple value inserts within a single INSERT statement. A simple construct is as follows –

```
INSERT INTO dbo.Persons (Name, Age)
VALUES ('Kumar', 35),
       ('Dave', 30)
```

You can do a double insert of data with one INSERT INTO statement using row constructors. Simply separate each group of values with a comma. The row constructor looks exactly like the double INSERT INTO except that you replace the INSERT with a comma. For a complete lesson on Row Constructors see Chapter 6 of Beginning SQL Joes 2 Pros Volume 1 ISBN: 1-4392-5317-X

The maximum number of rows that can be constructed using the table value constructor is 1000.

What is the new error handling mechanism started in SQL Server 2005?

Structured Error Handling in SQL Server is similar to the way we approach 'errors' in real life. When something does not go exactly as we expected, we adapt and find another way to accomplish our purpose. The job of a solution developer requires planning ahead and coding alternate pathways to keep our users and the application layer moving forward instead of stalling out when they encounter roadblocks. As analysts and application users, we have come to expect that application architects anticipate the majority of errors that our input could generate.

The TRY block is where you place code which you think may raise an error. A TRY block is a code segment starting with a BEGIN TRY statement and ending with END TRY. If a statement sits inside a TRY block and raises an error, then the error gets passed to another part of SQL Server and not to the client. The TRY block is aware that there is code which may fail.

The CATCH block serves as a contingency plan for failed code from the Try Block. In other words, if any statement raises a level 11 or higher severity in the TRY block, it will not show the error from the calling code. It will run the code you have set up in the CATCH block. For a complete lesson on SQL Error Handling see Chapter 10 of SQL Programming Joes 2 Pros Volume 4 ISBN: 1451579489

The TRY/CATCH construct is already present in many modern programming languages. TRY/CATCH helps to write logic to separate the action and error handling code. The code meant for the action is enclosed in the TRY block and the code for error handling is enclosed in the CATCH block. In case the code within the TRY block fails, the control automatically jumps to the CATCH block, letting the transaction roll back and resume execution. In addition to this, the CATCH block captures and provides error information that shows you the ID, message text, state, severity and transaction state of an error. (Read more here http://bit.ly/sqlinterview41).

What is the OUTPUT clause inside SQL Server?

The OUTPUT clause was introduced in SQL Server 2005, which is quite useful. The OUTPUT statement provides you with a confirmation copy of the records you just inserted, updated, deleted, or "upserted" using MERGE. The OUTPUT clause has access to inserted and deleted tables (virtual tables) just like triggers. The OUTPUT clause can be used to return values to the client clause. The OUTPUT clause can be used with INSERT, UPDATE, DELETE, or MERGE to identify the actual rows affected by these statements. For a complete lesson on the OUTPUT clause see Chapter 14 of SQL Queries Joes 2 Pros Volume 2 ISBN: 1-4392-5318-8

The OUTPUT clause can generate a table variable, a permanent table, or a temporary table. @@Identity will still work in SQL Server 2005, however you will find the OUTPUT clause very easy and powerful to use." This gets the audience excited about being empowered instead of taking the authors word for it. Here is an OUTPUT clause example (Read more here http://bit.ly/sqlinterview42).

What are table-valued parameters?

Table-valued parameters is a new feature introduced in SQL Server 2008. In earlier versions of SQL Server it was not possible to pass a table variable into a stored procedure as a parameter. In SQL SERVER 2008 we can use table-valued parameters to send multiple rows of data to a stored procedure or a function without creating a temporary table or passing in multiple parameters. Table-valued parameters are declared using user-defined table types. To use a table-valued Parameter we need to follow the steps shown below:

- Create a table type and define the table structure.
- Declare a stored procedure that has a parameter of table type.
- Declare a table type variable and reference the table type.
- Populate the variable using the INSERT statement.
- We can now pass the variable to the procedure. (Read more here http://bit.ly/sqlinterview43).

What is the use of data-tier application (DACPAC)?

The need for data-tier applications is to simplify development, deployment, and management of the database/data-tier objects that support multi-tier or client-server applications. DACPAC defines all of the database engine schema and instance objects, such as tables, views, and logins, required to support the application. The DAC operates as a single unit of

Pinal Dave / Vinod Kumar
SQLAuthority.com /ExtremeExperts.com

management through the development, deployment, and management lifecycle of the associated application. The DAC also contains policies that define the deployment prerequisites for the DAC.

A DAC can be deployed to instances of SQL Server 2008 R2 and SQL Azure.

What is RAID?

RAID (Redundant Array of Independent Disks) is a way of storing the same data in different places on multiple hard disks. By placing data on multiple disks, input/output operations can overlap in a balanced way, improving performance. The following are a few popular RAID type configurations used for database storage:

- RAID 0 – No Redundancy
- RAID 1 – Mirroring
- RAID 5 – Distributed Parity
- RAID 10 - Mirrored and Striped

What are the requirements of sub-queries?

- A sub-query must be enclosed in the parenthesis.
- A sub-query must be put on the right hand of the comparison operator.
- A sub-query cannot contain an ORDER BY clause.
- A query can contain more than one sub-query.

Pinal Dave / Vinod Kumar
SQLAuthority.com /ExtremeExperts.com

What are the different types of sub-queries?

- Single-row sub-query, where the sub-query returns only one row.
- Multiple-row sub-query, where the sub-query returns multiple rows.

What is PIVOT and UNPIVOT?

A pivot table can automatically sort, count, and total the data stored in one table or spreadsheet and create a second table displaying the summarized data. The PIVOT operator turns the values of a specified column into column names, effectively rotating a table. The UNPIVOT operator table is a reverse of the PIVOT operator. (To read more on this topic go here: http://bit.ly/sqlinterview44)

Can a stored procedure call itself or another recursive stored procedure? How many levels of stored procedure nesting are possible?

Yes, to the first question. As T-SQL supports recursion, you can write stored procedures that call themselves. Recursion can be defined as a method of problem solving wherein the solution is arrived at by repetitively applying it to subsets of the problem. A common application of recursive logic is to perform numeric computations that lend themselves to repetitive evaluation by the same processing steps. Stored procedures are nested when one stored procedure calls another or executes managed code by referencing a CLR routine, type, or aggregate. You can nest stored procedures and managed code references up to 32 levels.

Points to Ponder from SQL Architecture Basics Joes 2 Pros Volume 3 ISBN: 1451579462 (Joes2Pros.com)

1. A filegroup is a collection of datafiles which are managed as a single unit. SQL Server databases have a primary filegroup and may also have user defined secondary filegroups (like OrderHist).

2. You can only have one Primary filegroup per database but you can have as many user defined filegroups as you want.

3. Log files have a structure different from datafiles and cannot be placed into filegroups.

4. A schema is a namespace for database objects. In previous versions of SQL Server, database owners and schemas were conceptually the same object. Beginning in SQL Server 2005, owners and schemas are separate, and schemas serve as containers of objects.

5. A fully qualified name (FQN) is the complete object identifier. The FQN includes the server name, database name, schema name, and object name. The first three parts (server, database, and schema names) are known as the qualifiers of the object name, as they are used to differentiate the object from any other database object.

6. Database snapshots enable working with data as it appears at a point in time rather than reflecting the current status of the data. Snapshots are useful for reporting, development, and testing purposes.

7. The data portion of a row can contain the following elements:

   o   Fixed length data
   o   Null block

Pinal Dave / Vinod Kumar
SQLAuthority.com /ExtremeExperts.com

- o Variable block
- o Variable length data

8. The data type defines the characteristic of the data that is stored in a column. In addition to the system-supplied data types, user-defined data types can be created for specific needs. User defined data types are also called Alias types.

9. SQL Server 2008 has two specific spatial data types Geometry and Geography.

10. The Geography data type stores round-earth latitude and longitude earth coordinates that represent points, lines, and polygons.

11. The Geometry data type stores flat XY grid coordinates for points, lines, and polygons.

12. A clustered index determines the physical organization of data in the table. Each table can have only one clustered index.

13. When you create a primary key on a table, a clustered index is created by default unless you use the NONCLUSTERED argument.

14. You can put a nonclustered index on a heap or on a clustered table. Nonclustered indexes are useful when users require multiple ways to search for data.

15. You can implement nonclustered indices on heaps.

16. Nonclustered indices are automatically rebuilt when:
- o An existing clustered index on the table is dropped.
- o A clustered index on the table is created.
- o A column covered by the nonclustered index changes.

Common Tricky Questions

Success is not final, failure is not fatal: it is the courage to continue that counts - Winston Churchill

Which TCP/IP port does the SQL Server run on? How can it be changed?

SQL Server runs on port 1433. It can be changed from the SQL Server Configuration Manager -> SQL Server Network Configurations -> Protocols for SQL Server -> TCP/IP properties –> IP Addresses -> TCP Port number, both on the client and the server.

What are the differences between a clustered and a non-clustered index?

A clustered index is a special type of index that reorders the way records in the table are physically stored. Therefore, any given table can have only one clustered index. The leaf nodes of a clustered index contain the actual data. For a complete lesson on clustered and non-clustered indices see Chapter 8 of SQL Architecture Basics Joes 2 Pros Volume 3 ISBN: 1451579462

A non-clustered index is a special type of index in which the logical order of the index does not match the physical stored order of the rows on disk. The leaf node of a non-clustered index does not consist of the data pages. Instead, the leaf nodes contain index rows and a pointer to the data (clustered index key or RID). (Read more here http://bit.ly/sqlinterview45).

When is the use of the UPDATE STATISTICS command appropriate?

This command is basically used when a large amount of data is processed. If a large amount of deletions, modifications or bulk copies into the tables has occurred, it has to update the indices to take these changes into account. UPDATE STATISTICS updates the indices on these tables accordingly. For a complete lesson on SQL statistics see Chapter 12 of SQL Architecture Basics Joes 2 Pros Volume 3 ISBN: 1451579462

> You can use the DBCC SHOW_STATISTICS command to find out how current the tables statistics are.

What is SQL Profiler?

SQL Profiler is a graphical tool that allows system administrators to monitor events in an instance of Microsoft SQL Server. You can capture and save data about each event to a file or SQL Server table to analyze later. For example, you can monitor SQL Server in a production environment to see which stored procedures are executing very slowly and hampering performance.

Use SQL Profiler to monitor only the events in which you are interested. If traces are becoming too large, you can filter

Pinal Dave / Vinod Kumar
SQLAuthority.com /ExtremeExperts.com

them based on the information you want, so that only a subset of the event data is collected. Monitoring too many events adds overhead to the server and the monitoring process. This can cause the trace file or trace table to grow very large, especially when the monitoring process takes place over a long period of time.

In a production environment, enable server side trace to reduce the impact of collecting trace data.

What is SQL Server agent?

The SQL Server agent plays an important role in the day-to-day tasks of a database administrator (DBA). It is often overlooked as one of the main tools for SQL Server management. Its purpose is to ease the implementation of tasks for the DBA, with its full-function scheduling engine, which allows you to schedule your own jobs and scripts. (Read more here http://bit.ly/sqlinterview46)

SQL Server agent is not available with SQL Server Express editions.

What is BCP and when is it used?

BCP or "Bulk Copy Program" is a tool used to copy huge amounts of data from tables and views. BCP does not copy the complete structures from source to destination. The BULK INSERT command helps to import a data file into a database table or view in a user-specified format. For a complete lesson on BCP see Chapters 7 of Beginning SQL Joes 2 Pros Volume 1 ISBN: 1-4392-5317-X.

What are the authentication modes in SQL Server? How can it be changed?

There are two authentication modes in SQL Server.

- Windows mode
- Mixed mode – SQL and Windows

To change authentication mode in SQL Server, go to Start -> Programs- > Microsoft SQL Server and click SQL Server Management Studio and under *Object Explorer*, right-click the server, and then click *Properties*. On the *Security page*, under Server authentication, select the new server authentication mode, and then click OK. For a lesson on authentication modes in SQL Server see Chapters 10 of Beginning SQL Joes 2 Pros Volume 1 ISBN: 1-4392-5317-X.

Can you configure SQL Server without the SA account?

The SA account is a well-known guessable SQL Server account and is often targeted by malicious users. Do not enable the SA account unless your application requires it. With SQL Server 2008 R2 onwards, you can also rename the SA account.

If **Windows Authentication mode** is selected during installation, the SA login is disabled and a password is assigned by setup. If you later change authentication mode to **SQL Server and Windows Authentication mode**, the SA login remains disabled.

Which command using SQL Server Management Studio will give you the Version of SQL Server?

There will be times when you will need to locate metadata to learn something about SQL Server. For example, you may need to find out what version of SQL Server is running on a particular machine. (Imagine you need to run some queries using a loaner machine, or perhaps you are assisting a colleague with a query and need to see what version of SQL Server they are using.)

Metadata consists of data about that data. In other words, it describes the design of the table where you enter the employee data. It can also describe the settings and properties of your database or your instance of SQL Server. The ServerProperty( ) function can show a variety of properties for your server (e.g., ANSI null setting, language settings, etc.). We can use the ServerProperty( ) function to show the level of SQL Server running on a machine. SQL Server's product levels include Beta, RTC, or RTM

```
SELECT SERVERPROPERTY('Edition') AS Edition,
SERVERPROPERTY('ProductLevel') AS ProductLevel,
SERVERPROPERTY('ProductVersion') AS ProductVersion
GO
```

(Read more here http://bit.ly/sqlinterview47)

Pinal Dave / Vinod Kumar
SQLAuthority.com /ExtremeExperts.com

What is log shipping?

Log shipping is the process of automating the backup of database and transaction log files on a production SQL server with the goal of then restoring them onto a standby server.

In log shipping, the log file from one server is automatically updated to the backup database on the backup server. If one server fails, the other server will have the same transactions run and therefore the other db and can be used as a disaster recovery plan. The key feature of log shipping is that it will automatically backup transaction logs throughout the day and automatically restore them on the standby server at defined intervals.

Name a few ways to get an accurate count of the number of records in a table?

Using tables and catalog views:

```
SELECT * FROM table1;

SELECT COUNT(*) FROM table1;

SELECT rows FROM sysindexes
WHERE id = OBJECT_ID(table1) AND indid < 2
```

Using SQL Server 2008 DMVs:

```
SELECT object_name(i.object_id) as
objectName, i.[name] as indexName,
sum(p.rows) as rowCnt
```

Pinal Dave / Vinod Kumar
SQLAuthority.com /ExtremeExperts.com

```
FROM sys.indexes I
INNER JOIN sys.partitions p
  ON i.object_id = p.object_id AND
i.index_id = p.index_id
WHERE i.object_id =
object_id('dbo.table1')
  AND i.index_id <= 1
GROUP BY i.object_id, i.index_id, i.[name]
```

What does it mean to have the QUOTED_IDENTIFIER ON? What are the implications of having it OFF?

When SET QUOTED_IDENTIFIER is ON, identifiers can be delimited by double quotation marks, and literals must be delimited by single quotation marks. When SET QUOTED_IDENTIFIER is OFF, identifiers cannot be quoted and must follow all T-SQL rules for identifiers. (Read more here http://bit.ly/sqlinterview47)

What is the difference between a local temporary table and a global temporary table?

A *local* temporary table exists only for the duration of a connection, or if defined inside of a compound statement, for the duration of the compound statement.

A *global* temporary table remains in the database as long as connection exists. When that connection is closed, the global temporary table disappears. Unlike local temporary table global temporary table can be accessed while it exists from another connection.

What are table variables and how do they differ from local temporary tables?

A table variable is like a local temporary table but has some interesting differences. The scoping rules of table variables are the same as any other variable inside SQL Server. For example, if you define a variable inside a stored procedure, it can't be accessed outside the stored procedure:

- The table variable is NOT necessarily a memory resident. Under memory pressure, the pages belonging to a table variable can be pushed out to tempdb.

- Rollback doesn't affect table variables (unlike Temp tables). Table variables don't participate in transactions or locking.

- Any DML operation done on table variables is NOT logged.

- No statistics are maintained for a table variable which means - any changes in data impacting a table variable will not cause recompilation of queries accessing the table variable.

What is the STUFF function and how does it differ from the REPLACE Function?

The STUFF function is used to overwrite existing characters using this syntax: STUFF (string_expression, start, length, replacement_characters), where string_expression is the string that will have characters substituted. Start is the starting position, length is the number of characters in the string that are substituted, and replacement_characters are the new characters interjected into the string. The REPLACE function is used to replace existing characters of all

Pinal Dave / Vinod Kumar
SQLAuthority.com /ExtremeExperts.com

occurrences. Using the syntax REPLACE (string_expression, search_string, replacement_string), will replace every incident of search_string found in the string_expression with the replacement_string.

How do you get @@ERROR and @@ROWCOUNT at the same time?

If @@ROWCOUNT is checked after an error checking statement, then it will have 0 as the value of @@RECORDCOUNT since it would have been reset. If @@RECORDCOUNT is checked before the error-checking statement then @@Error would get reset. To get @@error and @@ROWCOUNT at the same time, include both in same statement and store them in a local variable like seen here:

```
SELECT @RC = @@ROWCOUNT, @ER = @@ERROR
```

A standard DECLARE statement (without value assignment) doesn't reset the @@ERROR.

What is a scheduled job and what is a scheduled task?

A scheduled task lets administrators automate processes that run on regular or predictable cycles as part of maintenance. A user can schedule administrative tasks, such as cube processing, to run during times of slow business activity. Users can also determine the order in which tasks run by creating job steps within a SQL Server Agent job, e.g. back up the database and update statistics of the tables. Job steps give users control over the flow of execution. If one job fails, then

Pinal Dave / Vinod Kumar
SQLAuthority.com /ExtremeExperts.com

the user can configure SQL Server Agent to continue to run the remaining tasks or to stop execution.

What are the advantages of using stored procedures?

- Stored procedures can reduce network traffic and latency, boosting application performance.
- Stored procedure execution plans can be reused; they stay cached in SQL Server's memory, reducing server overhead.
- Stored procedures help promote code reuse.
- Stored procedures can encapsulate logic. You can change stored procedure code without affecting clients.
- Stored procedures provide better security to your data.

What is a table called, if it has neither cluster nor non-cluster index?

A table that does not have a clustered index is referred to as a "heap" and a table that has a clustered index is referred to as a "clustered table." Microsoft Press Books and Books online (BOL) refers to a table without a clustered index as a heap. You can put a non-clustered index on a heap or on a clustered table. A table that has no indices is called an unindexed table.

A heap is a table that does not have a clustered index and therefore, the pages are not linked by pointers. The IAM pages are the only structures that link the pages in a table together. Unindexed tables are good for fast storing of data. Many times, it is better to drop all of the indexes from a table and then do a bulk INSERT and restore the indicies after that.

Can SQL Server be linked to other servers like Oracle?

SQL Server can be linked to any server provided it has an OLE-DB provider from Microsoft to allow a link, e.g. Oracle has an OLE-DB provider that Microsoft provides to add it as a linked server to the SQL Server group.

What command do we use to rename a database, a table, or a column?

To rename a database:

We can change the database name as follows:
sp_renamedb 'oldname' , 'newname'
If someone is using the database it will not accept sp_ renamedb. In that case, first bring the database to single user mode using sp_dboptions. Once ready, use sp_renamedb to rename the database. Use sp_dboptions to bring the database to multi-user mode. e.g.

```
USE master;
GO
EXEC sp_dboption AdventureWorks, 'Single User', True
GO
EXEC sp_renamedb 'AdventureWorks', 'AdvWorks_New'
GO
EXEC sp_dboption AdventureWorks, 'Single User', False
GO
```

Pinal Dave / Vinod Kumar
SQLAuthority.com /ExtremeExperts.com

Renaming a database requires membership in the sysadmin or dbcreator fixed server roles.

To Rename a Table

We can change the table name using sp_rename as follows:
sp_rename 'oldTableName' 'newTableName'

e.g.

SP_RENAME 'Table_First', 'Table_Last'
GO

To Rename a Column

The sp_Rename can be used to rename a column. For a lesson on sp_rename Joins see Chapters 7 of Beginning SQL Joes 2 Pros Volume 1 ISBN: 1-4392-5317-X

The script for renaming any column is as follows:
sp_rename 'TableName.[OldcolumnName]',
'NewColumnName', 'Column'
e.g.

sp_RENAME 'Table_First.Name', 'NameChange', 'COLUMN'
GO

Renaming objects, columns, and indices, requires the ALTER permission on the object. Renaming user types requires CONTROL permission on the type.

What are sp_configure commands and SET commands?

Use sp_configure to display or change server-level settings. To change the database-level settings, use ALTER DATABASE. To change settings that affect only the current user session, use the SET statement.

e.g.

```
sp_CONFIGURE 'show advanced', 0
GO
RECONFIGURE
GO
sp_CONFIGURE
GO
```

You can run the following command and check the advanced global configuration settings.

```
sp_CONFIGURE 'show advanced', 1
GO
RECONFIGURE
GO
sp_CONFIGURE
GO
```

(Read more here http://bit.ly/sqlinterview48)

Pinal Dave / Vinod Kumar
SQLAuthority.com /ExtremeExperts.com

How do you implement one-to-one, one-to-many and many-to-many relationships while designing tables?

One-to-one relationships can be implemented as a single table and rarely as two tables with primary and foreign key relationships. One-to-many relationships are implemented by splitting the data into two tables with primary key and foreign key relationships.

Many-to-many relationships are implemented using a junction table (sometimes called a bridge table) with the keys from both the tables forming the composite primary key of the junction table. For a lesson on many-to-many relationships see Chapter 2 of SQL Queries Joes 2 Pros Volume 2 ISBN: 1-4392-5318-8.

What is the difference between COMMIT and ROLLBACK when used in transactions?

The simplest way to describe the steps of a transaction is to use an example of updating an existing record into a table. When the insert runs, SQL Server gets the data from storage, such as a hard drive, and loads it into memory and your CPU. The data in memory is changed and then saved to the storage device. Finally, a message is sent confirming the rows that were affected.

When you transfer money from savings to checking, you are doing another explicit transaction. A transfer from savings to checking is actually two separate events. If you transfer $500 to checking, you expect to see a $500 withdrawal from savings and a $500 deposit to checking. Your bank would not call you

Pinal Dave / Vinod Kumar
SQLAuthority.com /ExtremeExperts.com

the next day to say they successfully withdrew $500 from savings, but did not credit your checking account.

By putting a series of DML statements between the BEGIN TRAN and COMMIT TRAN you ensure all statements succeed or fail as a single unit. Any failure means the final commit is never reached because the transaction is aborted. The records are never saved for storage in a database.

Encountering an error is one way to cause a running transaction to discard all of its changes. When the transaction does this, it is called rolling back the transaction. Sometimes you will intentionally rollback a transaction through code logic. The usual structure of the TRANSACTION is as follows:

BEGIN TRANSACTION
    <<Procedural / SET Operations>>
COMMIT TRANSACTION or ROLLBACK TRANSACTION

When COMMIT is executed, every statement between the BEGIN TRANSACTION and COMMIT TRANSACTION becomes persistent in the database. When rollback is executed, every statement between the BEGIN TRANSACTION and ROLLBACK TRANSACTION are reverted to the state before the BEGIN TRANSACTION was executed. For a lesson COMMIT and ROLLBACK see Chapter 9 of Beginning SQL Joes 2 Pros Volume 1 ISBN: 1-4392-5317-X

Pinal Dave / Vinod Kumar
SQLAuthority.com /ExtremeExperts.com

What is an execution plan? When would you use it? How would you view the execution plan?

An execution plan is a graphical or textual roadmap showing the data retrieval methods chosen by the SQL Server query optimizer for a stored procedure or ad-hoc query. The execution plan is a very useful tool for a developer to understand the performance characteristics of a query or stored procedure since the optimized plan is the one that SQL Server will place in its cache and use to execute the stored procedure or query. Within the SQL Server Management Studio, there is an option called "Include Actual Execution Plan" (or use CTRL+M shortcut) under the SQL Editor Toolbar. If this option is turned on, it will display the query execution plan in a separate window when the query is executed. For a lesson on execution plans see Chapter 10 of SQL Architecture Basics Joes 2 Pros Volume 3 ISBN: 1451579462

What is the CHECKPOINT process in SQL Server?

The CHECKPOINT process writes all in-memory dirty pages for the current database to disk. Dirty pages are data pages that have been entered into the buffer cache and modified, but not yet written to disk. When data is written to disk, SQL Server becomes aware when the response issues a checkpoint in the log for that transaction. Checkpoints save time during a later recovery by creating a point at which all dirty pages became persistent and guaranteed to have been written to disk.

The SHUTDOWN WITH NOWAIT statement shuts down SQL Server without executing a checkpoint in each database.

What is the difference between table aliases and column aliases? Do they affect performance?

Usually, when the name of the table or column is very long or complicated to write, aliases are used to refer them.

e.g.

```
SELECT VeryLongColumnName col1
FROM VeryLongTableName tab1
```

In the above example, col1 and tab1 are the column alias and table alias, respectively. They do not affect the performance at all. For a lesson on table aliases see Chapters 4 of Beginning SQL Joes 2 Pros Volume 1 ISBN: 1-4392-5317-X

Table alias can be accessed by any part of a SELECT clause, while *Column aliases* are set in the SELECT clause and can be accessed only in the ORDER BY clause.

What is the difference between CHAR and VARCHAR datatypes?

VARCHARs are variable length strings with a specified maximum length. If a string is less than the maximum length, then it is stored verbatim without any extra characters, e.g. names and emails. CHARS are fixed-length strings with a specified set length. If a string is less than the set length, then

Pinal Dave / Vinod Kumar
SQLAuthority.com /ExtremeExperts.com

it is padded with extra characters, e.g. phone number and zip codes. For instance, for a column which is declared as VARCHAR(30) and populated with the word *SQL Server*, only 10 bytes will be stored in it. However, if we have declared the column as CHAR(30) and populated with the word *SQL Server*, it will still occupy 30 bytes in the database. For a lesson on CHAR and VARCHAR datatypes see Chapter 3 of SQL Architecture Basics Joes 2 Pros Volume 3 ISBN: 1451579462

ROW / PAGE compressions can reduce space even for fixed length datatypes.

What is the difference between VARCHAR and VARCHAR(MAX) datatypes?

VARCHAR stores variable-length character data whose range varies up to 8000 bytes; varchar(MAX) stores variable-length character data whose range may vary beyond 8000 bytes and up to 2 GB.

The TEXT datatype and "Text in row" table option will be deprecated in future versions, and the usage of VARCHAR(MAX) is strongly recommended instead of TEXT datatypes.

VARCHAR(MAX) datatypes can be used inside triggers unlike the Text datatype. The VARCHAR(MAX) datatype can be used with normal string functions (LEN, Substring, Concatenation, as local variables etc).

Pinal Dave / Vinod Kumar
SQLAuthority.com / ExtremeExperts.com

What is the difference between VARCHAR and NVARCHAR datatypes?

In principle, they are the same and are handled in the same way by your application. The only difference is that NVARCHAR can handle unicode characters, allowing you to use multiple languages in the database (Arabian, Chinese etc.).

With Unicode data types (e.g., nchar, nvarchar, ntext), each character occupies 2 bytes. In SQL Server, a Unicode data type is generally denoted by an "n" or "N." When SQL Server generates code involving Unicode data, you see an "N" accompanying Unicode data throughout the script. NVARCHAR takes twice as much space when compared to VARCHAR. Use NVARCHAR only if you need localization or internationalization support.

Just like with regular character data (char, varchar), a blank space included in Unicode data (e.g., a space in a name [Joe Smith] or an address [1234 Main Street]) is counted as a character. For a lesson on datatypes see Chapter 3 of SQL Architecture Basics Joes 2 Pros Volume 3 ISBN: 1451579462

What are the important points to note when multilanguage data is stored in a Table?

There are two things to keep in mind while storing unicode data. First, the column must be of a unicode data type (nchar, nvarchar, ntext). Second, the value must be prefixed with N while insertion. For example,

```
INSERT INTO table (Hindi_col)
VALUES (N'हिंदी data')
```

Note: When SQL Server generates code involving Unicode data, you see an "N" accompanying Unicode data throughout the script.

Picking the right collation for the database, tempDB and all the variables used are critical when handling multiple languages inside SQL Server. (Read more here http://bit.ly/sqlinterview49)

How do you optimize stored procedures?

There are many tips and tricks for doing this. Here are a few:

- Include SET NOCOUNT ON statement.
- Use schema name with object name.
- Do not use the prefix "sp_" in the stored procedure name.
- Use IF EXISTS (SELECT 1) instead of (SELECT *).
- Use the sp_executesql stored procedure instead of the EXECUTE statement for Dynamic SQL.
- Try to avoid using SQL Server cursors whenever possible.
- Keep the transaction as short as possible.
- Use TRY/CATCH for error handling.
- Optimize queries and fine tune indexes.
- Use table variables and temp tables appropriately.

(Read more here http://bit.ly/sqlinterview50)

What is SQL injection? How do you protect against a SQL injection attack?

SQL injection is an attack in which malicious code is inserted into strings that are later passed to an instance of SQL Server for parsing and execution. Any procedure that constructs SQL statements should be reviewed for injection vulnerabilities because SQL Server will execute all syntactically valid queries that it receives. Even parameterized data can be manipulated by a skilled and determined attacker. Here are a few methods which can be used to protect again SQL Injection attack:

- Use type-safe SQL parameters.
- Use parameterized input with stored rocedures.
- Use the parameters collection with dynamic SQL.
- Use escape characters in the LIKE clause.
- Wrap parameters with QUOTENAME() and REPLACE()
- Validate ALL input elements. For un-structured data like XML documents, validate all data against a schema as it is entered.
- Never concatenate user input that is not validated. String concatenation is the primary point of entry for script injection.
- Always run the SPs under least amount of privileges to the database. Deny direct access to database objects.

Being vague and generic on Error Messages makes it difficult to progress with SQL injection attacks.

How do you find out the list schema name and table Name for the database?

We can use any of the following scripts:

```
SELECT '['+SCHEMA_NAME(schema_id) +
'].['+ Name +']' AS SchemaTable
FROM sys.tables

SELECT '['+ TABLE_SCHEMA +'].[' +
TABLE_NAME +']' AS SchemaTable
FROM INFORMATION_SCHEMA.TABLES
```

(Read more here http://bit.ly/sqlinterview51)

How does using a separate hard drive for several database objects improve performance right away?

Separating objects across different physical hard drives will increase the number of IOPS (Input/output Operations Per Second) that can be handled in parallel for the SQL Server instance. This is a deployment strategy done by the DBA. For a lesson on data files and log files see Chapter 1 of SQL Architecture Basics Joes 2 Pros Volume 3 ISBN: 1451579462

A non-clustered index and tempdb can be created on a separate disk to improve performance. (Read more here http://bit.ly/sqlinterview52)

How do you find the list of fixed hard drives and free space on the server?

We can use the following stored procedure to figure out the number of fixed drives (hard drives) a system has along with the free space on each of those drives.

```
EXEC master.dbo.xp_fixeddrives
```

Why can there be only one clustered index per table and not more?

A clustered index determines the physical order of data in a table. For example the store names in a shopping mall are not lined up in alphabetical order. In other words, Zales could be right next to Benetton. These two stores might occupy units 410 and 411. Thus, the stores in a mall are clustered by unit number. The clustered index represents the actual physical order of your data. To lay out the stores alphabetically would require you to build another mall essentially duplicating it. For a lesson on Indexes see Chapter 8 of SQL Architecture Basics Joes 2 Pros Volume 3 ISBN: 1451579462

As a fact, we all know that a set of data can only be stored in one physical order without completely duplicating the table; that is why only one clustered index per table is possible. (Read more here http://bit.ly/sqlinterview53)

What is the difference between line feed (\n) and carriage return (\r)?

Different operating systems have a different way of understanding a new line. Mac only understands '\r' as a new line, while Unix and Linux understand '\n' as a new line character. Our favorite OS (Windows) needs both the characters together to interpret a new line, which is '\r\n'. This is the reason why a file created in one OS does not open properly in another OS and makes it messy.

In the code below you might wonder how a CHAR(2) can be equal to a CHAR(13). The reality is that these can represent special characters. The 10 represents a Line Feed and 13 the Carriage Return as seen below.

Line Feed – LF – \n – 0x0a – 10 (decimal)
Carriage Return – CR – \r – 0x0D – 13 (decimal)

```
DECLARE @NewLineChar AS CHAR(2)
= CHAR(13) + CHAR(10)
PRINT ('SELECT FirstLine AS FL '
+@NewLineChar +
'SELECT SecondLine AS SL' )
```

(Read more here http://bit.ly/sqlinterview54)

What is a HINT?

Hints are options and strong suggestions specified for enforcement by the SQL Server query processor on DML statements. The hints override any execution plan the query optimizer might select for a query. (Read more here http://bit.ly/sqlinterview55)

There are three different types of hints. Let us understand the basics of each of them separately.

Pinal Dave / Vinod Kumar
SQLAuthority.com /ExtremeExperts.com

Join hint

This hint is used when more than one table is used in a query. Two or more tables can be joined using different types of joins. This hint forces the type of join algorithm (INNER [LOOP | MERGE | JOIN] JOIN) that is used. Joins can be used in SELECT, UPDATE and DELETE statements. Note: since insert statements can only go against one table at a time they don't use any type of join.

Query hint

This hint is used when a certain kind of logic has to be applied to a whole query. Any hint used in the query is applied to the complete query as opposed to a part of it. There is no way to specify that only a certain part of a query should be used with the hint. After any query, the OPTION clause is specified to apply the logic to this query. A query always has any of the following statements: SELECT, UPDATE, DELETE, INSERT or MERGE (SQL 2008); and this hint can be applied to all of them. For a lesson on query hints see Chapter 10 of SQL Architecture Basics Joes 2 Pros Volume 3 ISBN: 1451579462

Table hint

This type of hint is used when certain kinds of locking mechanisms of tables has to be controlled. The SQL Server query optimizer always puts the appropriate kind of lock on tables, when any of the Transact SQL operations SELECT, UPDATE, DELETE, INSERT or MERGE is used. There are certain

Pinal Dave / Vinod Kumar
SQLAuthority.com /ExtremeExperts.com

cases when the developer knows when and where to override the default behavior of the locking algorithm, and these hints are useful in those scenarios. (Read more here http://bit.ly/sqlinterview56)

> The SQL Server query optimizer typically selects the best execution plan for a query, so use HINTs with caution.

How do you delete duplicate rows?

We can delete duplicate rows using a CTE (Common Table Expression) with the ROW_NUMBER () feature of SQL Server 2005 and SQL Server 2008.

e.g.

```
WITH CTE (COl1,Col2, DuplicateCount)
AS
(
SELECT COl1,Col2,
ROW_NUMBER() OVER(PARTITION BY COl1,Col2 ORDER BY
Col1) AS DuplicateCount
FROM DuplicateRcordTable
)
DELETE
FROM CTE
WHERE DuplicateCount >1
```

(Read more here http://bit.ly/sqlinterview58)

Pinal Dave / Vinod Kumar
SQLAuthority.com /ExtremeExperts.com

Why does the LOGON trigger fire multiple times during a single login in SSMS?

This happens because multiple SQL Server services are running and also because SQL Server Management Studio Intellisense is turned on. If you have Object Explorer open in a separate query window, then this will also open additional connections to SQL server causing SQL to log these additional open connections. (Read more here http://bit.ly/sqlinterview57)

What are aggregate functions?

Aggregate functions perform a calculation on a set of values and return a single value. Aggregate functions ignore NULL values (except for the COUNT function). The HAVING clause is used, along with GROUP BY for filtering a query using aggregate values.

The following functions are some of the aggregate functions.
AVG, MIN, CHECKSUM_AGG, SUM, COUNT, STDEV, COUNT_BIG, STDEVP, GROUPING, VAR, MAX, VARP (Read more here http://bit.ly/sqlinterview59)

When working with aggregate functions, keep an eye on your result set. By trying to show too much detail, you can inadvertently undo the good effect the aggregate function has in your report. For example if you group total sales by EmployeeID you would get one number per employee. If you grouped on EmployeeID and Data then you would get daily totals for each employee. This would give you the same employee listed many times.

Pinal Dave / Vinod Kumar
SQLAuthority.com /ExtremeExperts.com

Count(*) is another use of Count() function and counts all records, including nulls. Count(Fieldname) counts the number of records found where that field is not null. Count(*) will count all records found in any fields (even if they are null). For a lesson on aggregated functions see chapter 4 of SQL Queries Joes 2 Pros Volume 2 ISBN: 1-4392-5318-8

What is the use of @@ SPID in SQL Server?

A SPID is the Server Process ID of the current user connection. And using that session ID, we can find out the SPID that the last query was executed. (Read more here http://bit.ly/sqlinterview60)

What is the difference between an index seek and an index scan?

A scan is the scenario we described earlier where you look at every item before selecting. This is not always bad, especially with small lists you intend to analyze thoroughly. When you go to a new restaurant, you want to look over all the items before deciding. This will take longer as the list you must scan gets bigger. However, in a large list where you know what you are looking for, a scan of every item becomes a big waste of time and you probably wish the list had been better organized.

An index scan means that SQL Server reads all rows in a table, and then returns only those rows that satisfy the search criteria. When an index scan is performed, all the rows in the leaf level of the index are scanned. This essentially means that all the rows of the index are examined instead of the table directly. This is sometimes compared to a table scan, in which all the table data is read directly. However, there is usually little difference between an index scan and a table scan.

Access to heap data will always result in a table scan.

An index seek, on the other hand, means that the Query Optimizer relies entirely on the index leaf data to locate rows satisfying the query condition. An index seek will be most beneficial in cases where a small percentage of rows will be returned. For a lesson on Seeks and Scans see Chapter 8 of SQL Architecture Basics Joes 2 Pros Volume 3 ISBN: 1451579462.

An index seek will only affect the rows that satisfy a query condition and the pages that contain these qualifying rows; in terms of performance, this is highly beneficial when a table has a very large number of rows and you want to return a very small percentage of those row in your query. (Read more here http://bit.ly/sqlinterview61)

What is the maximum size per database for SQL Server Express?

SQL Server Express supports a maximum size of 4 GB per database, which excludes all the log files. From SQL Server 2008 R2 onwards this size has been increased to 10GB. This is quite a bit of data for a conventional application and when designed properly it can be used efficiently for small development purposes. (Read more here http://bit.ly/sqlinterview62)

How do we know if any query is retrieving a lot or very little data?

In one way, it is quite easy to figure this out by just looking at the result set; however, this method cannot be relied upon every time as it is difficult to reach a conclusion when there are many columns and many rows.

It is easy to measure how much data is retrieved from server to client side. SQL Server Management Studio has a feature that can measure client statistics. (Read more here http://bit.ly/sqlinterview63)

How do you create a primary key with a specific name while creating a table?

An alternate syntax for adding a primary key in your CREATE TABLE statement can create constraints while creating a new table using the CREATE TABLE statement. For a lesson on creating table level constraints see chapters 1 of SQL Programming Joes 2 Pros Volume 4 ISBN: 1451579489

```
CREATE TABLE [dbo].[TestTable] (
[ID] [int] IDENTITY(1,1) NOT NULL,
[FirstName] [varchar](100) NULL,
CONSTRAINT [PK_TestTable] PRIMARY KEY CLUSTERED
([ID] ASC))
GO
```

(Read more here http://bit.ly/sqlinterview64)

Pinal Dave / Vinod Kumar
SQLAuthority.com /ExtremeExperts.com

What is the T-SQL code to take a database offline and to bring a database online?

```
-- Take the Database Offline
ALTER DATABASE [myDB] SET OFFLINE WITH
ROLLBACK IMMEDIATE
GO
```

```
-- Take the Database Online
ALTER DATABASE [myDB] SET ONLINE
GO
```

(Read more here http://bit.ly/sqlinterview65)

Can we insert data if the clustered Index is disabled?

No, we cannot insert data if the clustered index is disabled because clustered indexes are in fact original tables which are physically ordered according to one or more keys (columns). (Read more here http://bit.ly/sqlinterview66)

How do you RECOMPILE a stored procedure at run-time?

We can use a RECOMPILE hint with a query and recompile only that particular query. However, if the parameters are used in many statements in the stored procedure and we want to recompile all the statements, then instead of using the RECOMPILE option with a query, we have a better option that uses the WITH RECOMPILE hint during stored procedure creation or execution. We can RECOMPILE the stored procedure in two ways.

Pinal Dave / Vinod Kumar

Option 1:

CREATE PROCEDURE dbo.PersonAge @MinAge INT, @MaxAge INT
WITH RECOMPILE
AS
SELECT*
FROM dbo.tblPerson
WHERE Age >= @MinAge AND Age <= @MaxAge
GO

Option 2:

EXEC dbo.PersonAge 65, 70 **WITH RECOMPILE**

SQL Server also has statement level recompilation that can be forced using the OPTION (Recompile) construct.

This OPTION (RECOMPILE) construct method is not recommended for large stored procedures because the recompilation of so many statements may outweigh the benefit of a better execution plan. (Read more here http://bit.ly/sqlinterview67)

Describe performance differences between IF EXISTS (Select null from table) and IF EXISTS (Select 1 from table).

When you write "select null", it will still return 4 bytes of memory on a 32-bit machine for the return value.

Pinal Dave / Vinod Kumar
SQLAuthority.com /ExtremeExperts.com

And when you are returning 1 byte or 2 bytes, you end up taking 4 bytes of memory because of the padding to keep memory aligned.

So there is no performance difference between IF EXISTS (Select null from table) and IF EXISTS (Select 1 from table). (Read more here http://bit.ly/sqlinterview68)

What is the difference in the performance between INSERT TOP (N) INTO Table and using TOP with INSERT?

INSERT TOP (N) INTO Table is faster than Using Top with INSERT but when we use INSERT TOP (N) INTO Table, the ORDER BY clause is totally ignored. (Read more here http://bit.ly/sqlinterview69)

Does the order of columns in UPDATE Statements matter?

No, the order of columns in an UPDATE statement does not matter. Both the options below produce the same results.

Option 1:
UPDATE TableName
SET Col1 ='Value', Col2 ='Value2'

Option 2:
UPDATE TableName
SET Col2 ='Value2', Col1 ='Value'

(Read more here http://bit.ly/sqlinterview70)

Points to Ponder from SQL Programming Joes 2 Pros Volume 4 ISBN: 1451579489 (Joes2Pros.com)

1. Data integrity is the consistency and accuracy of the data which is stored in a database. A constraint performs data validation to help maintain database integrity by preventing invalid data from being entered.

2. You can create constraints using:
   o The CONSTRAINT keyword in the CREATE TABLE statement at the time you create the table.
   o The CONSTRAINT keyword in the ALTER TABLE statement after you have created the table.

3. Primary keys cannot accept null values, but unique indexes can accept 1 null value.

4. A check constraint restricts the values that users can enter into a particular column during INSERT and UPDATE statements.

5. You can temporarily disable a CHECK constraint. However, data integrity will not be enforced while the constraint is disabled.

6. Foreign keys are constraints that compare values between one column and another. Setting up a foreign key relationship enforces what is known as referential integrity.

7. If you don't want to check the existing data at the time you create the foreign key, then specify WITH NOCHECK.

8. A trigger is a special type of stored procedure that is not called directly by a user. A DML trigger is like a stored proc that executes when an INSERT, UPDATE, or DELETE event modifies data in a table.

9. There are two categories of triggers.
- o After Triggers – executed after the INSERT, UPDATE, or DELETE is performed. You can only define these on tables. AFTER triggers can be specified for tables but not for views.
- o Instead of Triggers – are executed in place of the usual triggering action. Unlike AFTER triggers, INSTEAD OF triggers can be specified for both tables and views.

10. Much like constraints, it is possible to enforce data integrity through triggers. However, you should use constraints whenever possible.

11. A TRUNCATE TABLE statement run against a table will un-populate that table. However, no DML triggers will be fired off since TRUNCATE is a DDL statement.

12. What are the special memory resident tables available when dealing with triggers? Most people answer "Inserted, Updated, and Deleted." However, there are only two tables: Inserted and Deleted.

13. A nested trigger is a trigger which executes a statement that causes an AFTER trigger to fire again.

14. A view is a virtual table whose contents are defined by a query. Views are database objects and are stored in your database, similar to tables, stored procedures, and functions.

15. The tables that make up a view are called "base tables."

16. Views do not maintain separate copies of data. Therefore, when you are modifying records in a view, you are really modifying the records in the underlying base table.

Pinal Dave / Vinod Kumar
SQLAuthority.com /ExtremeExperts.com

17. A stored procedure is a named database object consisting of one or more lines of code. T-SQL statements run together in a single execution. A stored procedure is precompiled code that can be reused. You can also define your own custom stored procedures.

18. Table-valued parameters are new in SQL Server 2008. Table-valued parameters are a great way to pass in multiple rows of data at once, instead of just one value at a time.

19. A function is a SQL object stored in a database and consisting of T-SQL code that accepts parameters.

20. A user-defined function is a routine that you can create to accept parameters, perform a task, and return a result set.

21. Functions are similar to stored procedures in the way they work, but you must call a function using a SELECT statement or a WHERE clause within a SELECT statement.

22. If you want your procedure to raise an error defined by your own conditions, and this is not a system error, then you can call the RAISERROR( ) function. The first parameter can be a message number, text or a local @ variable. The message number corresponds to the message_id column in the sys.messages table.

23. If you use RAISERROR and specify text without a message number, you will get a message number of 50,000.

24. If you specify the message number and not the text, then you will get text belonging to the message as listed in the Sys.Messages table.

25. You can't manually raise errors below 13000. Those may be raised only by the system.

 Pinal Dave / Vinod Kumar
SQLAuthority.com /ExtremeExperts.com

Miscellaneous Questions on SQL SERVER 2008

If you can't make it good, at least make it look good.-Bill Gates

What are the basic uses for master, MSDB, model, tempdb and resource databases?

The **Master** *database* holds information for all the databases located on the SQL Server instance, and it is the glue that holds the engine together. Because SQL Server cannot start without a functioning master database, you must administer this database with care.

The **MSDB** *database* stores information regarding database backups, SQL Agent information, DTS packages, SQL Server jobs, PBM information and some replication information such as for log shipping.

The **tempdb** holds temporary objects such as global and local temporary tables and is a very important database for the instance. It is also the database that stores the version store when snapshot isolations are used. Each time SQL Server restarts the tempdb is copied from the model database.

Pinal Dave / Vinod Kumar
SQLAuthority.com /ExtremeExperts.com

Auto shrink is not allowed for **tempdb**. SQL Server 2008 R2 introduces **CHECKSUM** for tempdb.

The **model** *database* is essentially a template database used in the creation of any new user database created in the instance.

The **resource** *database* is a read-only database that contains all the system objects that are included in SQL Server. SQL Server system objects such as sys.objects are physically persisted in the resource database, but they logically appear in the sys schema of every database. The resource database does not contain user data or user metadata.

SQL Server cannot back up the resource database via maintenance plans or normal backup commands. Perform your own file-based backup by treating the mssqlsystemresource.mdf file as if it were any other binary file.

What is the maximum number of indices per table?

SQL versions up to SQL Server 2005:

1 clustered Index + 249 nonclustered Indices = 250 Indices.

For SQL Server 2008 and onwards:

1 clustered index + 999 nonclustered Indices = 1000 Indices.
(Read more here http://bit.ly/sqlinterview71)

Explain a few of the new features of SQL Server 2008 Management Studio.

In SQL Server 2008 Microsoft has upgraded SSMS with many new features as well as added tons of new functionalities requested by DBAs for a long time. A few of the important new features are as follows:

- IntelliSense for query editing
- MultiServer query
- Query editor regions
- Object Explorer enhancements
- Activity monitors

Explain IntelliSense for query editing:

After implementing IntelliSense, we don't have to remember all the syntax or browse online references. IntelliSense offers a few additional features besides just completing the keyword and giving options for object names to complete the query. (i.e. auto-completing database objects, highlighting incorrect syntax, etc).

Explain MultiServer query:

SSMS 2008 has a feature to run a query on different servers from one query editor window. First of all, make sure that you have registered all of the servers under Registered Server. Once they are registered, right click on the server group name and click New Query. For example: To obtain server version information from multiple servers run the following query as a

Pinal Dave / Vinod Kumar
SQLAuthority.com /ExtremeExperts.com

MultiServer query. The queries below will give you the results of every server registered in your SSMS.

```
SELECT
SERVERPROPERTY('Edition') AS Edition,
SERVERPROPERTY('ProductLevel') AS ProductLevel,
SERVERPROPERTY('ProductVersion') AS ProductVersion
```

(Read more here: http://bit.ly/sqlinterview129)

Explain query editor regions:

When T-SQL code contains hundreds of lines, then after a while it becomes more and more confusing. The regions are defined by the following hierarchy:

From the first GO command to the next GO command. Statements between BEGIN – END, BEGIN TRY – END TRY, BEGIN CATCH – END CATCH.

CREATE DDL statements like CREATE PROC form regions and XML tag regions are also available when you view XML columns.

Explain Object Explorer enhancements:

In Object Explorer Detail, the new feature is Object Search. Enter any object name in the object search box and the searched result will be displayed in the same window as the Object Explorer Detail.

Additionally, there are new wizards which help you perform several tasks, from policy management to disk monitoring.

Another cool feature is that everything displayed in the object explorer details screen can instantly copied and pasted to Excel without any formatting issue.

Explain activity monitors:

There are four graphs
- % Processor Time
- Waiting Tasks
- Database I/O
- Batch Requests/Sec

All four tabs provide very important information; however, the one which I refer to most is "Recent Expensive Queries." Whenever I find my server running slowly or having any performance-related issues, my first reaction is to open this tab and see which query is running slowly. I usually look at the query with the highest number for its average duration. The Recent Expensive Queries feature monitors the slowest queries that are in the SQL Server cache at that moment. (Read more here http://bit.ly/sqlinterview72)

Debugging capability was introduced with SQL Server 2008 Management Studio.

What is Service Broker?

Service Broker is a message-queuing technology in SQL Server that allows developers to integrate SQL Server fully into distributed applications. Service Broker is a feature which provides functionality to SQL Server to be able to send asynchronous, transactional messages. It allows a database to send a message to another database without waiting for the response; so the application will continue to function if the remote database is temporarily unavailable. (Read more here http://bit.ly/sqlinterview73)

What does the TOP operator do?

TOP is a row-limiter and helps you limit the number of records affected by your DML statement. For a lesson on the TOP keyword see Chapter 6 of SQL Queries Joes 2 Pros Volume 2 ISBN: 1-4392-5318-8

The TOP operator is used to specify the number of rows to be returned by a query. The TOP operator has a new addition in SQL SERVER 2008 that allows it to accept variables as well as literal values. The TOP operator can be used with INSERT, UPDATE, and DELETE statements.

> To use a variable / expression with the TOP operator it must be written inside parenthesis.

What is a CTE?

A CTE is the abbreviation for *Common Table Expression*. The CTE was one of the standout debut features in SQL Server 2005 and was widely applauded by SQL Server developers. Readers who are learning SQL Server now can be grateful they don't need to experience the pain and pitfalls of temporary tables (a.k.a., *temp tables*, which are different from derived tables) and other messy constructs whose work is now

Pinal Dave / Vinod Kumar
SQLAuthority.com /ExtremeExperts.com

elegantly accomplished by the CTE. Here is an example of the code to create a CTE:

```
WITH HighGrants AS
   (SELECT GrantID, GrantName, Amount
   FROM [Grant]
   WHERE Amount > 20000)
SELECT * FROM HighGrants
```

A CTE is an expression that can be thought of as a temporary result set which is defined within the execution of a single SQL statement. A CTE is similar to a derived table in that it is not stored as an object and lasts only for the duration of the query. (Read more here http://bit.ly/sqlinterview74)

Like derived tables, CTE's also require a SELECT statement to invoke them. However, with the CTE your SELECT statement appears beneath the code. The Common Table Expression features a clean looking query at the bottom because it handles all of the calculations and declarations at the top. For a lesson on Common Table Expressions see Chapters 9 of SQL Queries Joes 2 Pros Volume 2 ISBN: 1-4392-5318-8

A CTE can reference itself, thereby creating a recursive CTE. A recursive CTE is one in which an initial CTE is repeatedly executed to return subsets of data until the complete result set is obtained. For a lesson on recursive CTE's see Chapter 10 of SQL Queries Joes 2 Pros Volume 2 ISBN: 1-4392-5318-8.

A recursive CTE contains 3 elements:

- An initializer – Located in the anchor query of the CTE, this is the starting point of the data.
- Recursive – This is where initializer feeds the data for recursion.
- Termination – defines when the recursion must end.

We can limit the number of recursion levels allowed for a CTE statement by using the MAXRECURSION hint and a value between 0 and 32,767 in the OPTION clause.

What are some advantages of using a CTE?

- Using a CTE improves readability and enables easy maintenance of complex queries.
- The query can be divided into separate, simple, and logical building blocks, which can then be used to build more complex CTE's until the final result set is generated.
- The CTE makes writing recursive code in T-SQL significantly easier than it was in previous versions of SQL Server.
- A CTE can be defined in functions, stored procedures, triggers or even views.
- After a CTE is defined, it can be used as a table or a view and can SELECT, INSERT, UPDATE or DELETE Data.

Can we rewrite sub-queries into simple select statements using joins and CTEs?

Yes. We can rewrite sub-queries using the Common Table Expression (CTE). A Common Table Expression (CTE) is an expression that can be thought of as a temporary result set which is defined within the execution of a single SQL statement. A CTE is similar to a derived table in that it is not stored as an object and lasts only for the duration of the query.

e.g.

```
USE AdventureWorks
GO
WITH EmployeeDepartment_CTE AS (
SELECT EmployeeID,DepartmentID,ShiftID
FROM HumanResources.EmployeeDepartmentHistory)

SELECT ecte.EmployeeId,
ed.DepartmentID,                    ed.Name,ecte.ShiftID
FROM HumanResources.Department ed
INNER JOIN EmployeeDepartment_CTE ecte
ON ecte.DepartmentID = ed.DepartmentID
GO
```

What does the MERGE statement do?

The MERGE statement is new to SQL Server 2008 and is an excellent tool for handling table data. For years, database professionals have used the informal term *Upsert* with respect to bringing new data into an existing table. If the record is brand new, you want your query logic to insert that entire record into the table. However, if the record already exists, you want your query to compare the old record with the new record and update only the incremental changes. That logical process has been formalized as the MERGE statement.

MERGE is a new feature that provides an efficient way to perform multiple DML operations in a single statement. In previous versions of SQL Server, we had to write separate statements to INSERT, UPDATE, or DELETE data based on certain conditions, but now, using a MERGE statement, we can include the logic of such data modifications in one statement that even checks when the data is matched, then just update the matched record, and when unmatched, insert it. For a lesson on using MERGE see Chapter 13 of SQL Queries Joes 2 Pros Volume 2 ISBN: 1-4392-5318-8.

One of the most important advantages of the MERGE statement is all the data is read and processed only once. (Read more here http://bit.ly/sqlinterview75)

While using the MERGE statement, take a look at the code written on DML TRIGGERS (if any), because these need to operate on a set of rows rather than a single row.

What are the new data types introduced in SQL SERVER 2008?

The GEOMETRY datatype: The GEOMETRY datatype is a system .NET common language runtime (CLR) datatype in SQL Server. This datatype represents data in a two-dimensional

Euclidean coordinate system. For a lesson on the GEOMETRY datatype see Chapter 5 of SQL Architecture Basics Joes 2 Pros Volume 3 ISBN: 1451579462.

The GEOGRAPHY datatype: The GEOGRAPHY and GEOMETRY datatype is a system .NET common language runtime (CLR) datatype in SQL Server. Many of the functions are the same as with GEOMETRY but GEOMETRY does have a few functions not found in the GEOGRAPHY datatype. Another difference between the two is that when you specify GEOGRAPHY, you are usually specifying points in terms of latitude and longitude. For a lesson on the GEOGRAPHY datatype see Chapter 5 of SQL Architecture Basics Joes 2 Pros Volume 3 ISBN: 1451579462.

SQL Server 2008 supports an out-of-box a set of methods for the **geometry** spatial data type. These include methods defined by the Open Geospatial Consortium (OGC) standard and a set of Microsoft extensions to that standard.

New DATE and DATETIME datatypes: SQL Server 2008 introduces four new data types related to date and time: DATE, TIME, DATETIMEOFFSET, and DATETIME2. For a lesson on date and time datatypes see Chapter 4 of SQL Architecture Basics Joes 2 Pros Volume 3 ISBN: 1451579462.

- **DATE:** The new DATE datatype just stores the date itself. It is based on the Gregorian calendar and handles years from 1 to 9999.

DATE datatype - Uses only 3-bytes (fixed) for storage of this data.

- **TIME:** The new TIME (*n*) datatype stores time with a range of 00:00:00.0000000 through 23:59:59.9999999. TIME supports seconds down to 100 nanoseconds. Precision setting changes are allowed with this datatype. The *n* in TIME(*n*) defines this level of fractional second precision from 0 to 7 digits of precision.

To support the new date and time data types SQL Server 2008 introduces new functions SYSDATETIME, SYSUTCDATETIME, SYSDATETIMEOFFSET, SWITCHOFFSET, and TODATETIMEOFFSET.

- **The DATETIMEOFFSET datatype:** DATETIMEOFFSET (*n*) is the time-zone-aware version of the datetime datatype. The name will appear less odd when you consider what it really is: a date + time + time-zone offset. The offset is based on how far behind or ahead you are from Coordinated Universal Time (UTC) time.

- **The DATETIME2 datatype:** It is an extension of the DATETIME datatype in earlier versions of SQL Server. This new datatype has a date range covering dates from January 1 of year 1 through December 31 of year 9999. DATETIME2 not only includes the larger date range, but also has a timestamp and the same

Pinal Dave / Vinod Kumar
SQLAuthority.com /ExtremeExperts.com

fractional precision that TIME datatype provides (down to 100 nanoseconds).

The standard DATETIME datatype could store data January 1, 1753, through December 31, 9999 and had accuracy for time rounded to increments of .000, .003, or .007 seconds.

What is CLR (Common Language Runtime)?

The .NET framework can run managed code because it has the CLR. If SQL Server wanted to run managed code in its own environment, it would need its own .NET runtime. The SQL CLR is the engine SQL Server uses to run .NET code. SQL has its own built-in CLR. The SQL CLR runs managed code for SQL Server. In SQL Server 2005 and beyond, SQL Server objects such as user-defined functions can be created using such CLR languages. For a lesson on SQL CLR see Chapter 9 of SQL Interoperability Joes 2 Pros Volume 5 ISBN: 1-4515-7950-0.

This CLR language support extends not only to user-defined functions, but also to stored procedures and triggers. You can develop such CLR add-ons to SQL Server using Visual Studio. (Read more here http://bit.ly/sqlinterview76)

SQL Server 2008 lifts the limitation of CLR UDTs from 8000 bytes to 2GB.

Define HIERARCHYID datatypes?

The new HIERARCHYID datatype in SQL Server 2008 is a system-supplied CLR UDT that can be useful for storing and manipulating hierarchies. It is internally stored as a VARBINARY that represents the position of the current node in the hierarchy. You can create indexes, query nodes, add siblings etc. just like any other data inside SQL Server.

What are table types and table-valued parameters?

SQL Server 2008 introduces this new concept. *Table datatypes* save a table definition in the database and can be used later to define table variables or parameters. Because table datatypes let you reuse a table definition, they ensure consistency and reduce the chances for errors.

We can now use table datatypes for stored procedure and function input parameters. Using table datatypes as parameters is why they are called *Table-Valued Parameters* (TVP). A common scenario where TVPs are very useful is passing an "array" of keys to a stored procedure.

TVPs are read only in SQL Server 2008, and must be defined by using the READONLY keyword.

What are synonyms?

Also known as aliases, synonyms give you the ability to provide alternate names for database objects. For a lesson on Aliasing see Chapter 1 of Beginning SQL Joes 2 Pros Volume 1 ISBN: 1-4392-5317-X

You can alias object names; for example, you can alias the Employee table as Emp. You can also shorten names. This is especially useful when dealing with three and four part names; for example, shortening server.database.owner.object to object. (Read more here http://bit.ly/sqlinterview77).

Simply alias the table name as another name in the FROM clause and then reuse the shorter name. Here is a SQL example:

```
SELECT *
FROM Location AS Loc INNER JOIN Employee
AS Emp
ON Loc.LocationID = Emp.LocationID
```

What is LINQ?

Language Integrated Query (LINQ) adds the ability to query objects using .NET languages. The LINQ to SQL object/relational mapping (O/RM) framework provides the following basic features:

- Tools to create classes (usually called *entities*) mapped to database tables.
- Compatibility with LINQ's standard query operations.
- The DataContext class with features such as entity record monitoring, automatic SQL statement generation, record concurrency detection, and much more.

What are isolation levels?

Transactions specify an isolation level that defines the degree to which one transaction must be isolated from a resource or data modifications made by other transactions. Isolation levels

Pinal Dave / Vinod Kumar
SQLAuthority.com /ExtremeExperts.com

are described in terms of which concurrency side-effects, such as if *dirty reads* or *phantom reads*, and *lost updates* are allowed.

Transaction isolation levels control the following:

- Whether locks are taken when data is read, and what type of locks are requested.
- How long the read locks are held.
- Whether a read operation is referencing rows modified by another transaction.
    1. blocks until the exclusive lock on the row is freed.
    2. retrieves the committed version of the row that existed at the time the statement or transaction started, and reads the uncommitted data modification.

(Read more here http://bit.ly/sqlinterview78)

SQL Server has an additional isolation called SNAPSHOT.

How can you handle errors in SQL SERVER 2008?

Ever since SQL 2005 SQL Server supports the use of TRY/CATCH constructs. This is for providing structured error handling. SQL Server introduced new and improved options for error handling beginning with SQL Server 2005. Prior versions did not include structured error handling. Structured error handling in SQL Server is similar to the way we approach

Pinal Dave / Vinod Kumar
SQLAuthority.com /ExtremeExperts.com

errors in real life. When something does not go exactly as we expected, we adapt and find other ways to accomplish our goals. For a lesson on TRY/CATCH blocks see Chapter 10 of SQL Programming Joes 2 Pros Volume 4 ISBN: 1451579489.

The job of a solution developer requires planning ahead and coding alternate pathways to keep our users and the application layer moving forward instead of stalling out when they encounter roadblocks. As analysts and application users, we have come to expect that application architects anticipate the majority of errors which our input could generate. Bugs which block the user from proceeding, or which force the user to exit and re-enter the application, are severe problems which should be caught and remedied during the test cycle.

TRY/CATCH blocks lets us build error handling at the level we need, in the way we need to by setting a region where if any error occurs, it will break out of the region and head to an error handler. The TRY block is where you place code which you think may raise an error. A TRY block is a code segment starting with a BEGIN TRY statement and ending with END TRY statement. If a statement sits inside a TRY block and raises an error, then the error gets passed to another part of SQL Server and not to the client. The TRY Block is aware that there is code which may fail.

The CATCH block serves as a contingency plan for failed code from the TRY block. In other words, if any statement raises a non-critical level 11 or higher severity error in the TRY block, it will not show the error from the calling code. It will run the code you have set up in the CATCH block. The basic structure is as follows:

```
BEGIN TRY
<code>
END TRY
BEGIN CATCH
<code>
END CATCH
```

Errors that have a severity of 10 or lower / 20 or higher that cause the database engine to close the connection will not be handled by the TRY/CATCH block.

What are some of the salient behaviors of the TRY/CATCH block?

When an error condition is detected in a T-SQL statement that is inside a TRY block, control is passed to the CATCH block where the error can be processed:

- If there are no errors inside the TRY block, control passes to the statement immediately after the associated END CATCH statement.
- A TRY block must be followed immediately by a CATCH block.
- Each TRY block is associated with only one CATCH block.
- Each TRY/CATCH construct must be inside a single batch. We cannot place a TRY block in one batch and the associated CATCH block in another batch.
- TRY/CATCH constructs can be nested.

- ERROR_PROCEDURE() returns the name of the stored procedure or trigger where the error occurred.

Object name resolution errors and compile errors such as syntax errors that prevent a batch from executing are not caught in CATCH block.

What is RAISEERROR?

SQL Server will raise errors when the code you have written cannot or should not execute. For example, a table should not be created if one with the same name already exists. Suppose you have a stored procedure named UpdateOneEmployee which changes one employee record at a time. The logic of this stored procedure will allow you to potentially update two employees with the same info. If it was against company policy to update more than one employee record at a time, it's extremely unlikely that anyone would ever attempt to update multiple records at once. However, because SQL Server has no restriction against updating one or many records in one transaction, you want to add a layer of protection to help enforce company policy. This is a case where you don't want SQL Server to allow this update, even though SQL Server doesn't define it as an error. To accomplish this goal, you can raise your own error message based on conditions which you define. For a lesson on RAISERROR blocks see Chapter 10 of SQL Programming Joes 2 Pros Volume 4 ISBN: 1451579489.

Pinal Dave / Vinod Kumar
SQLAuthority.com /ExtremeExperts.com

RAISERROR generates an error message and initiates error processing for the session. RAISERROR can either reference a user-defined message stored in the **sys.messages** catalog view or build a message dynamically. The message is returned as a server error message to the calling application or to an associated CATCH block of a TRY/CATCH construct. (Read more here http://bit.ly/sqlinterview79)

The old style syntax for RAISERROR (*Format: RAISERROR integer string*) syntax is deprecated.

What is the XML datatype?

Integers hold numbers with no decimal points, varchars hold strings of varying length, and the Geography datatype holds a position on the earth. Introduced in SQL Server 2005, the XML datatype holds and understands valid XML streams.

The **xml** datatype lets you store XML documents and XML fragments in a SQL Server database. An XML fragment is an XML instance that has a missing single top-level *root* element. You can create columns and variables of the **xml** datatype and store XML instances in them. The **xml** datatype and associated methods help integrate XML into the relational framework of SQL Server. For a lesson on the XML datatype see Chapter 5 SQL of Interoperability Joes 2 Pros Volume 5 ISBN: 1-4515-7950-0

What is XPath?

XPath uses a set of expressions to select nodes to be processed. The most common expression that you'll use is the

Pinal Dave / Vinod Kumar SQLAuthority.com /ExtremeExperts.com location path expression, which returns back a set of nodes called a *node set*. XPath can use both an unabbreviated and abbreviated syntax. The following is the unabbreviated syntax for a location path:

/axisName::nodeTest[predicate]/axisName::nodeTest[predicate]

For a lesson on XPath and XQuery see SQL of Interoperability Joes 2 Pros Volume 5 ISBN: 1-4515-7950-0

What is typed XML?

We can create variables, parameters, and columns of the xml datatype - if we associate a collection of XML schemas with a variable, parameter, or column of xml datatype. In this case, the xml datatype instance is called typed XML. The fundamental advantage of using *typed XML* is we can perform some amount of validation constraint and even perform datatype validations.

How can you find tables without indexes?

Run the following query in the Query Editor.

```
USE <database_name>;
GO
SELECT SCHEMA_NAME(schema_id) AS schema_name
    ,name AS table_name
FROM sys.tables
WHERE OBJECTPROPERTY(OBJECT_ID,'IsIndexed') = 0
ORDER BY schema_name, table_name;
GO
```

How do you find the index size of a table?

We can use the following query to find the size of the index.

EXEC sp_spaceused [HumanResources.Shift]
(Read more here http://bit.ly/sqlinterview80)

How do you copy data from one table to another table?

There are multiple ways to do this.

1) *INSERT INTO SELECT*

This method is used when the table was already created in the database earlier and data has to be inserted into this table from another table. If columns listed in the INSERT clause and SELECT clause are the same, listing them is not required.

2) *SELECT INTO*

This method is used when the target table was not created earlier and it needs to be created when data from one table must be inserted into a newly created table from another table. The new table will be created using the same data types as those in selected columns. (Read more here http://bit.ly/sqlinterview81)

What are some of the limitations of SELECT...INTO clause?

We would highly recommend using INSERT...INTO...SELECT to copy data to another table. Some of the limitations for the SELECT...INTO syntax are:

- You cannot specify a table variable or table-valued parameter as the new table.

- The FILESTREAM attribute does not transfer to the new table.
- Creates a new table in the default filegroup. SELECT...INTO does not use the partition scheme of the source table.
- Indexes, constraints, and triggers defined in the source table are not transferred to the new table.
- When a computed column is included in the select list, the corresponding column in the new table is not a computed column.
- The user running SELECT *field list* INTO requires the CREATE TABLE permission.

What is Filestream in SQL Server?

Filestream allows you to store unstructured large objects (text documents, images, and videos) in the file system and have these files integrated within the database. Filestream basically integrates the SQL Server Database Engine with NTFS (New Technology File System); it basically stores the data in the varbinary(max) datatype. Using this datatype, the unstructured data is stored in the NTFS file system, and the SQL Server Database Engine manages the link between the Filestream column and the actual file located in the NTFS. Using Transact-SQL statements users can insert, update, delete and select the data stored in Filestream-enabled tables.

Filestream data is not encrypted even when transparent data encryption is enabled.

SQLAuthority.com /ExtremeExperts.com
Pinal Dave / Vinod Kumar

What are some of the caveats in working with the Filestream datatype?

Here are some of the interesting considerations with the Filestream datatype:

- The sizes of the BLOBs are limited only by the volume size of the NTFS file system.
- Filestream data must be stored in Filestream filegroups.
- Filestream filegroups can be on compressed volumes.
- We can use all backup and recovery models with Filestream data, and the Filestream data is backed up with the structured data
- When using failover clustering, the Filestream filegroups must be on shared disk resources.
- Encryption is not supported on Filestream data.
- SQL Server does not support database snapshots for Filestream filegroups.
- Database mirroring does not support Filestream but log shipping and replication support Filestream datatypes.

The 10-GB database size limit from SQL Server 2008R2 Express does not include the Filestream data container. It used to be 4GB in the previous versions of SQL Express.

What do you mean by TABLESAMPLE?

TABLESAMPLE allows you to extract a sampling of rows from a table in the FROM clause. The rows retrieved are random and they are not in any order. This sampling can be based on a percentage of number of rows. You can use TABLESAMPLE when only a sampling of rows is necessary for the application instead of the full result set. (Read more here http://bit.ly/sqlinterview82)

What are ranking functions?

Ranking functions return a ranking value for each row in a partition. All the ranking functions are non-deterministic. For a lesson on Ranking Function see Chapter 7 of SQL Queries Joes 2 Pros Volume 2 ISBN: 1-4392-5318-8.

Each of the ranking functions also needs the OVER( ) clause. The different ranking functions are as follows:

ROW_NUMBER () OVER ([<partition_by_clause>]
<order_by_clause>)
Returns the sequential number of a row within a partition of a result set, starting at 1 for the first row in each partition.

RANK () OVER ([<partition_by_clause>] <order_by_clause>)
Returns the rank of each row within the partition of a result set. After a tie there will numeric gaps in the next ranked number.

DENSE_RANK () OVER ([<partition_by_clause>]
<order_by_clause>)
Returns the rank of rows within the partition of a result set, without any gaps in the ranking.

NTILE (integer_expression) OVER ([<partition_by_clause>]
<order_by_clause>)

Pinal Dave / Vinod Kumar
SQLAuthority.com /ExtremeExperts.com

Distributes the rows in an ordered partition into a specified number of groups.

(Read more here http://bit.ly/sqlinterview83)

What is ROW_NUMBER()?

ROW_NUMBER() returns a column as an expression that contains the row's number within the result set. This is only a number used in the context of the result set; if the result changes, the ROW_NUMBER() will change.

What is a ROLLUP Clause?

The ROLLUP clause is used to do aggregate operations on multiple levels in hierarchy. If we want a sum on different levels without adding any new columns, then we can do it easily by using ROLLUP. We have to just add the WITH ROLLUP clause in the GROUP BY clause. (Read more here http://bit.ly/sqlinterview84)

How can I track the changes or identify the latest INSERT-UPDATE-DELETE statements from a table?

In SQL Server 2005 and earlier versions, there was no built in functionality to determine which row was recently changed and what the changes were. Prior to SQL Server 2008, the most common way to see changed data was with triggers send data into archive tables that had similar fields to the tables you needed to track. However, in SQL Server 2008, a new feature known as Change Data Capture (CDC) has been introduced to capture the changed data. (Read more here http://bit.ly/sqlinterview86)

Pinal Dave / Vinod Kumar
SQLAuthority.com /ExtremeExperts.com

What is Change Data Capture (CDC) in SQL Server 2008?

Another innovative new feature in SQL Server 2008 is Change Data Capture (abbreviated as CDC). The concept is similar to Change Tracking but with a major difference. CDC tracks every field in your table(s) – not just the primary key fields. For a lesson on CDC see Chapter 12 of SQL Programming Joes 2 Pros Volume 4 ISBN: 1451579489.

Change Data Capture (CDC) records INSERTs, UPDATEs, and DELETEs applied to SQL Server tables and makes a record available of what changed, where, and when. The changed records in CDC are presented in simple relational *change tables* rather than in an esoteric chopped salad of XML. These changed tables contain columns that reflect the column structure of the source table you have chosen to track along with the metadata needed to understand the changes that have been made. (Read more here http://bit.ly/sqlinterview85)

What is change tracking inside SQL Server?

Change Tracking is a new and much anticipated feature in SQL Server 2008. Prior to SQL Server 2008, SQL DBAs had to code complex triggers and archive tables in order to track changes made to their database tables. For a lesson on Change Tracking see Chapter 11 of SQL Programming Joes 2 Pros Volume 4 ISBN: 1451579489.

Change tracking in SQL Server 2008 enables applications to obtain only changes that have been made to the user tables, along with some information about those changes. With

Pinal Dave / Vinod Kumar
SQLAuthority.com /ExtremeExperts.com

change tracking integrated into SQL Server, complicated custom change tracking solutions no longer have to be developed.

How is change tracking different from change data capture?

CDC tracks all fields in the table whereas change tracking only tracks the changes to the primary key of the table. The tracking mechanism in change data capture involves an asynchronous capture of changes from the transaction log so that changes are available after the DML operation. In change tracking, the tracking mechanism involves synchronous tracking of changes in line with DML operations so that change information is available immediately. In change data capture historical data is tracked and in change tracking historical data is not tracked.

What is auditing inside SQL Server?

SQL Server audit offers features that help DBAs achieve their goals of meeting regulatory compliance requirements. SQL Server audit provides centralized storage of audit logs and integration with system center. SQL Server audit was designed with the following primary goals in mind:

- Security – The audit feature, and its objects, must be truly secure.
- Performance – Performance impact must be minimized.
- Management – The audit feature must be easy to manage.

- Discoverability - Audit-centric questions must be easy to answer.

How is auditing different from change data capture?

CDC was created to help ETL scenarios by providing support for incremental data load. It uses an asynchronous capture mechanism that reads the transaction log and populates change capture tables with the row data and provides API's that provide access to that captured data in a number of ways. CDC is not to be used for auditing purposes.

Use SQL Server auditing as a compliance need. These are some of the basic differences of CDC over SQL Server audits:

- Audits cannot / must not have an option to be altered by any mechanism.
- CDC can be purged based on the retention period.
- SQL Server audits can also keep track of SELECT statements.
- Audits can also track server changes, login failures, DBCC commands execution.

How do you get data from a database on another server?

If you want to import data only through a T-SQL query, then use the OPENDATASOURCE function. To repeatedly get data from another server, create a linked server and then use the OPENQUERY function or use 4-part naming. If you are not using T-SQL, then it is better to use the import/export wizard, and you can save it as a SSIS package for future use. (Read more here http://bit.ly/sqlinterview87)

Pinal Dave / Vinod Kumar
SQLAuthority.com /ExtremeExperts.com

What is the bookmark lookup and RID lookup?

When a small number of rows are requested by a query, the SQL Server optimizer will try to use a non-clustered index on the column or columns contained in the WHERE clause to retrieve the data requested by the query. If the query requests data from columns not present in the non-clustered index, then the SQL Server must go back to the data pages to get the data in those columns.

In the above scenario, if a table has a clustered index, it is called **bookmark lookup** (or key lookup); if the table does not have a clustered index (heap), it is called a RID lookup. (Read more here http://bit.ly/sqlinterview88)

Lookups are expensive, hence consider using the INCLUDE clause to make covering indexes.

What is the difference between GETDATE() and SYSDATETIME() in SQL Server 2008?

With the GETDATE() function, the precision is in milliseconds, and with the SYSDATETIME() function, the precision is down to 100 nanoseconds.
(Read more here http://bit.ly/sqlinterview89)

What is the difference between the GETUTCDATE and SYSUTCDATETIME functions?

These functions return data as UTC time (Coordinated Universal Time). In case of the GETUTCDATE(), the precision is in milliseconds. SYSUTCDATETIME() has a default precision of

7 digits after the seconds (aka nanoseconds). For a lesson on date and time datatypes see Chapter 4 of SQL Architecture Basics Joes 2 Pros Volume 3 ISBN: 1451579462.

SYSDATETIME( ), SYSUTCDATE( ), and SYSDATETIMEOFFSET( ) can be assigned to a variable in any one of the date and time datatypes.

How do you check if automatic statistic update is enabled for a database?

The following query can be used to determine if Automatic Statistic update is enabled:

```
SELECT is_auto_create_stats_on,
is_auto_update_stats_on
FROM sys.databases
WHERE name ='YOUR DATABASE NAME HERE'
```

(Read more here http://bit.ly/sqlinterview90)

What is the difference between a seek predicate and a predicate?

The seek predicate is the operation that describes the b-tree portion of the seek. Predicate is the operation that describes the additional filter using non-key columns. Based on the description, it is very clear that the seek predicate is better than the predicate as it searches indices, whereas in predicate, the search is on a non-key a column – which implies that the search is on the data in page within the table itself. (Read more here http://bit.ly/sqlinterview91)

What are various limitations of views?

- The ORDER BY clause does not work in a view unless it is used with the TOP keyword. (Read more here http://bit.ly/sqlinterview92)

- The SQL Server engine always selects the optimal execution plan. In most of the cases where the index created on the view is not the optimal index then the SQL Server engine has to fall back on its base tables and their indexes to come up with an optimal execution plan. Creating indexes on views is a practice not used very often and is commonly avoided on most systems. (Read more here http://bit.ly/sqlinterview94)

- Once the view is created and if the basic table has any column added or removed, it is not usually reflected in the view until it is refreshed. (Read more here http://bit.ly/sqlinterview95)

- One of the most prominent limitations of the view is that it does not support COUNT (*); however, it can support COUNT_BIG (*). (Read more here http://bit.ly/sqlinterview96)

What are the limitations of indexed views?

For a lesson on Indexed Views see Chapter 5 of SQL Programming Joes 2 Pros Volume 4 ISBN: 1451579489.

Some of the limitations with Indexed views are:

- The UNION operation is not allowed in an indexed view. (Read more here http://bit.ly/sqlinterview97)

- We cannot create an Index on a nested view scenario which means we cannot create index on a view built from

Pinal Dave / Vinod Kumar
SQLAuthority.com /ExtremeExperts.com

another view. (Read more here http://bit.ly/sqlinterview98)

- SELF JOINs are not allowed in indexed view. (Read more here http://bit.ly/sqlinterview99)
- OUTER JOINS are not allowed in an indexed view. (Read more here http://bit.ly/sqlinterview100)
- Cross database queries are not allowed in indexed views. (Read more here http://bit.ly/sqlinterview101)
- The view must be created using the WITH SCHEMABINDING option.
- ANSI_NULLS needs to be set for all existing tables that will be referenced in the view.
- Indexed views cannot contain text, ntext, image, filestream, or xml columns.

What is a covered index?

A covered index can satisfy a query just by its index keys without having the need to touch any data pages. When an Index covers the query in this way it is a called covering index. It means that when a query is fired, SQL Server doesn't need to go to the table to retrieve the rows, but can produce the results directly from the index as the index covers all the columns used in query. (Read more here http://bit.ly/sqlinterview102)

When I delete data from a table, does SQL Server reduce the size of that table?

When data is deleted from any table, SQL Server does not reduce the size of the table right away; however, it marks those pages as free pages, showing that they belong to the

Pinal Dave / Vinod Kumar
SQLAuthority.com /ExtremeExperts.com

table. When new data is inserted, they are put into those free pages first. Once those pages are filled up, SQL Server will allocate new pages. If you wait for some time, the background process de-allocates the pages, finally reducing the page size. (Read more here http://bit.ly/sqlinterview103)

Points to Ponder from SQL of Interoperability Joes 2 Pros Volume 5 ISBN: 1-4515-7950-0 (Joes2Pros.com)

1. Metadata is data about your data. Metadata is information which helps to describe the properties and relationships of data.

2. Text files only contain data (no metadata). It's up to you to understand what the data means. XML is self-describing data, as it contains both data and metadata.

3. The FOR XML clause instructs SQL Server to return data as an XML stream rather than a rowset. The FOR XML clause is appended at the end of your SELECT statement.

4. The RAW option can be used with the ROOT or ELEMENTS keywords or both to customize your expected XML stream. The ROOT and ELEMENTS keywords are optional.

5. Raw and Auto modes both can use the ELEMENTS option. If ELEMENTS is not used, then both Raw and Auto will display your XML stream in attributes.

6. Path mode queries recognize a syntax called XPath to easily customize the layout.

7. SQL Server can turn table data into XML data. SQL Server can turn XML data into tabular data. XML shredding is the process of extracting data from XML streams and turning them into a tabular stream (e.g., a table).

8. Before you can process an XML document with T-SQL, you must parse the XML into a tree representation of the various nodes and store it within SQL Server's internal cache using the sp_XML_PrepareDocument stored procedure.

9. The XML data type has a built-in method called query( ) which allows you to query for the parts of the XML you need.

10. XQuery was created primarily as a query language for getting data stored in an XML form.

11. XQuery is a query and functional programming language that is designed to query collections of XML data. The main purpose of XQuery is to get information out of XML databases.

12. XQuery is also capable of manipulating XML data by updating, inserting, and deleting data or elements. XPath is a subset of XQuery.

13. In SQL Server 2005 & 2008, the XML data type provides five methods:
   o query( ) – used to extract XML fragments from an XML data type.
   o value( ) – used to extract a single value from an XML document.
   o exist( ) – used to determine if a specified node exists. Returns 1 if it does exist, returns 0 if it doesn't exist.
   o modify( ) – updates XML data in an XML data type.
   o nodes( ) – shreds XML data into multiple rows.

14. Referencing relational columns in your XML field is known as "binding" the relational column.

Pinal Dave / Vinod Kumar
SQLAuthority.com /ExtremeExperts.com

15. An executable (.exe) file is known as an "out of process" assembly. Out of process assemblies contain enough information to launch or run on their own. An assembly whose extension ends in .dll is known as an "in process" assembly.

16. SQL Server supports the use of in-process assemblies (DLL's) through the SQL CLR.

17. PowerShell goes beyond the cmd.exe shell that ships with windows. PowerShell is Microsoft's automation framework and command-line shell built on top of the .NET Framework.

18. SQL PowerShell is a shell that sends commands to SQL Server.

19. It's expected that, in the future, all Microsoft applications running on the Windows platform will be PowerShell aware.

20. PowerShell can run most of the old shell commands like dir, cd, and cls but also has its own commands that appear as a verb-noun combination.

21. PowerShell is made up of a command-line shell and its associated scripting language. Windows PowerShell talks to and is integrated with the Microsoft .NET Framework.

22. Windows PowerShell 2.0 was released with Windows 7 and Windows Server 2008 R2. This was released to manufacturing in August 2009.

23. Installing SQL in your system also installs new PowerShell Cmdlets.

24. The most used SQL PowerShell Cmdlet is Invoke-Sqlcmd.

DBA Skills Related Questions

If you want to test your memory, try to recall what you were worrying about one year ago today.- E. Joseph Cossman

How do you rebuild the master database?

The master database is a system database that contains information about the server's running configuration. When SQL Server 2005 is installed, it usually creates master, model, msdb, tempdb, resourcedb, and the distribution system database by default. Without the master database, SQL Server cannot be started. This is the reason why it is extremely important to back up the master database.

To rebuild the master database, run setup.exe, verify, and repair the SQL Server instance, and rebuild the system databases. This procedure is most often used to rebuild the master database for a corrupted installation of SQL Server. (Read more here http://bit.ly/sqlinterview104)

What are standby servers? Explain the types of standby servers.

A standby server is a type of server that can be brought online in a situation when the primary server goes offline. This is useful for when an application needs continuous (high) availability from the server. There is always a need to set up a mechanism where data and objects from the primary server are moved to a secondary (*standby*) server. This mechanism usually involves the process of moving a backup from the primary server to the secondary server using T-SQL scripts. Often, database wizards are used to set up this process.

The different types of standby servers are given as follows:

1) Hot standby:

A hot standby can be achieved in SQL Server using SQL Server 2005 Enterprise Edition or later versions of SQL Server Enterprise. SQL Server 2005 introduced database mirroring to be able to configure automatic failover in a disaster recovery scenario. When using of synchronous mirroring, the database is replicated to both servers simultaneously. This is a little more expensive but provides the highest availability. In this case, both primary and standby servers have identical data all times.

2) Warm standby:

In warm standby, automatic failover is not configured. This is usually set up using log shipping or asynchronous mirroring. Sometimes a warm standby will lag by a few minutes or seconds, which results in the loss of a few of the latest updates when the primary server fails and the secondary server needs to come online. Sometimes a warm standby

Pinal Dave / Vinod Kumar
SQLAuthority.com /ExtremeExperts.com

server that is lagging by a few transactions is brought back to the current state by applying the most recent transaction log.

3) Cold standby:

Cold standby servers need to be switched manually, and sometimes all the backups as well as the required OS needs to be applied. A cold standby just physically replaces the previous server.

(Read more here http://bit.ly/sqlinterview105)

What is the difference between GRANT and WITH GRANT while giving permissions to the user?

When using GRANT, the principal cannot grant the same permission to other users. On the other hand, when using WITH GRANT, the principal will be able to give the same permission to other users. (Read more here http://bit.ly/sqlinterview106)

A table-level DENY does not take precedence over a column-level GRANT.

How do you copy tables, schemas, and views from one SQL Server to another?

There are multiple ways to do this:

1) "Detach database" from one server and "attach database" to another server.

2) Manually script all of the objects using SSMS and run the script on a new server.

3) Use the Move Database Wizard of SSMS. (Read more here http://bit.ly/sqlinterview107)

Where are SQL Server usernames and passwords stored in SQL Server?

The system catalog views of sys.server_principals and sys.sql_logins can show the various users in the system. These are stored in the master database.

What is SQLCMD?

SQLCMD is an enhanced version of isql and osql, and it provides more functionality than the other two options. In other words, SQLCMD is a better replacement of isql (which will be deprecated eventually) and osql (not included in SQL Server 2005 RTM). For a lesson on SQLCMD see Chapter 6 of Beginning SQL Joes 2 Pros Volume 1 ISBN: 1-4392-5317-X.

SQLCMD can work in two modes - i) BATCH and ii) interactive modes. (Read more here http://bit.ly/sqlinterview108)

What is Utility Control Point (UCP)?

The SQL Server utility models an organization's SQL Server-related entities in a unified view. Utility Explorer and SQL Server Utility viewpoints in (SSMS) provide administrators a holistic view of resource health through an instance of SQL Server that serves as a Utility Control Point (UCP). The UCP collects configuration and performance information from managed instances of SQL Server every 15 minutes by default.

To remove an instance of SQL Server from Utility Control Point, make sure that the SQL Server and SQL Server Agent services are running on the instance to remove.

What can be monitored via UCP?

Entities that can be viewed in SQL Server UCP include:

- Instances of SQL Server.
- Data-tier applications.
- Database files.
- Storage volumes.

Resource utilization dimensions that can be viewed in SQL Server UCP include:

- CPU utilization.
- Storage space utilization.

Some of the current restrictions include:

- The Instance has to be a SQL Server relational engine.
- It must be a SQL 2008 R2 or a SQL 2008 SP2 instance.
- UCP cannot be done for Express editions.
- It must operate within a single Windows domain, or across domains with two-way trust relationships.

How is SQLCMD different from OSQL?

The SQLCMD utility is a command prompt utility to run adhoc T-SQL statements and scripts. You can also run SQLCMD interactively. SQLCMD is the new choice for scripting with SQL Server. There are interesting extended options which make SQLCMD worth using, like using the –A for DAC Dedicated Administrative Connections.

SQLAuthority.com /ExtremeExperts.com
Pinal Dave / Vinod Kumar

SSMS uses the Microsoft .NET Framework SqlClient for execution in regular and SQLCMD mode in Query Editor. When SQLCMD is run from the command line, SQLCMD uses the OLE DB provider.

What is the data collector?

SQL Server 2008 introduced the concept of the data collector. You can obtain and save data that is gathered from several sources about the health of your SQL Server. The data collector provides data collection containers that you can use to determine the scope and frequency of data collection on a SQL Server system. The data collector provides predefined collector types that you can use for data collection. The out-of-box collector types are:

- Generic T-SQL query collector type
- Generic SQL trace collector type
- Performance counters collector type
- Query activity collector type

What system data collection sets are predefined inside SQL Server?

During the installation, there are 3 system data collections that are made available to DBAs. These are to be later configured to monitor SQL Server. These cannot be deleted:

- **Disk usage**: Collects data about disk and log usage for all the databases installed on the system.
- **Server activity**: Collects resource usage statistics and performance data from the server and SQL Server.

147
Pinal Dave / Vinod Kumar
SQLAuthority.com /ExtremeExperts.com

- **Query statistics**: Collects query statistics, individual query text, query plans, and specific queries.

The data collector uses the role-based security model implemented by SQL Server Agent.

When will you use the SQLDiag tool?

The SQLdiag utility is a general purpose diagnostics collection utility that can be run as a console application or as a service and can be very useful for performance tuning exercises. SQLdiag is fully configurable through the SQLdiag.xml configuration file and can collect a variety of diagnostic information like Windows performance logs, Windows event logs, SQL Server Profiler traces, SQL Server blocking information, and SQL Server configuration information.

Introduced in SQL Server 2005 edition this replaces the PSS Diag utility used by the CSS team (Customer Support Services team).

What is the use of the Dedicated Admin Connection (DAC)?

The Dedicated Admin Connection allows users to connect to SQL server when normal connection attempts fail, for example, when the server is out of memory, hanging, or other bad states that means it is not responding to normal connection requests. A DAC is achieved by pre-allocating dedicated resources during server startup, including memory and scheduler etc.

Pinal Dave / Vinod Kumar
SQLAuthority.com /ExtremeExperts.com

How do you invoke a DAC connection?

There are two fundamental ways of connecting to the DAC –

- You can use SQLCMD which is the command prompt version and the osql version in SQL Server 2005 and newer. We have a new option **-A** which enables the connection to be an admin connection.

- To enable the admin connection from SSMS you need to use the **ADMIN:** prefix before your server's name in the logon screen. For example if your SQL server were named Reno you would enter *ADMIN: Reno* on the server name text box of the *"Connect to Server"* dialog box.

> SQL Server Express does not listen on the DAC port unless started with a trace flag 7806.

When would you use a server-side trace?

Running Profiler in a production environment is not a recommended practice on any day. To minimize this overhead, server side tracing via SQL trace system stored procedures can be used but must also be done with care.

> After you start a server-side trace, the trace continues to run and generates output until you stop the trace.

What are the SP's used for creating, starting and stopping a server-side trace?

The following are the system SPs that we can use to work with a server-side trace:

- sp_trace_create - Creates a trace definition.
- sp_trace_setevent - Alters an event or event column to a trace.
- sp_trace_setfilter - Applies a filter to a trace.
- sp_trace_setstatus - Starts, stops, and close traces.
- sp_trace_generateevent - Creates a user-defined event.

What are the events of a default trace?

The default SQL Server trace from SQL Server 2005 onwards is a background trace that runs continuously and records event information that can be useful in troubleshooting problems. Though the list is long, the following are captured by the default trace:

- Data file auto grow
- Data file auto shrink
- Database mirroring status change
- Log file auto grow
- Log file auto shrink
- Error log
- Missing column statistics
- Missing join predicate
- Object altered
- Object created
- Object deleted
- Server memory change

Apart from these there are many other SQL Server security auditing events also captured like: Add DB user event, DBCC

Pinal Dave / Vinod Kumar
SQLAuthority.com /ExtremeExperts.com

event, login failed, backup/restore event, server starts and stops, and many more.

What is central management inside SQL Server?

SQL Server 2008 introduced a new method of administering multiple servers by enabling you to designate a central management server. An instance of SQL Server that is designated as a central management server maintains a list of registered servers. A typical scenario for a DBA is to write a single query across multiple servers to determine the version of all the servers in a single result set using a single query.

Transact-SQL statements and policy-based management policies can be executed at the same time against server groups.

What tools are available for extended events?

For the SQL Server engine, XEvent is configured using a series of T-SQL statements. There is no graphical tool support for XEvent in the current version of SQL Server 2008 R2. There are no tools provided allowing you to view the results of XEvent targets except those provided by Windows to view ETW data (ETW = Event Tracing for Windows). Note: Event tracing for Windows is the standard way to trace all features used by Windows.

How do you disable an index?

ALTERINDEX [IndexName] ON TableName DISABLE

GO

How do you enable an index?

ALTERINDEX [IndexName] ON TableName REBUILD

GO

(Read more here http://bit.ly/sqlinterview109)

What is data compression?

In SQL SERVER 2008, data compression comes in three major flavors:

- Row compression
- Page compression
- Dictionary compression

Row compression

Row compression changes the format of the physical storage of data. It minimizes the metadata (column information, length, offsets etc.) associated with each record. Numeric data types and fixed-length strings are stored in variable-length storage format, just like Varchar. (Read more here http://bit.ly/sqlinterview110)

NVarchar(max) data is never compressed even if it is stored in the row.

Page Compression

Page compression allows common data to be shared between rows for a given page. It uses the following techniques to compress data:

- Row compression.
- Prefix compression. For every column in a page, duplicate prefixes are identified. These prefixes are saved in compression information headers which reside in the page header. A reference number is assigned to these prefixes and that reference number is replaced wherever those prefixes are being used.

Dictionary compression

Dictionary compression searches for duplicate values throughout the page and stores them in a Clustered Index. The main difference between prefix and dictionary compression is that the former is only restricted to one column while the latter is applicable to the complete page.

SQL Server 2008 R2 brings support for compression on Unicode data.

What are wait types?

There are three types of Wait Types, namely:

Resource waits. Resource waits occur when a worker requests access to a resource that is not available because that

Pinal Dave / Vinod Kumar
SQLAuthority.com /ExtremeExperts.com

resource is either currently used by another worker thread or it's not yet available.

Queue waits - Queue waits occur when a worker thread is idle, waiting for work to be assigned.

External waits - External waits occur when a SQL Server worker thread is waiting for an external event. (Read more here http://bit.ly/sqlinterview111). For a lesson on Advanced Wait Stats Concepts see book Joes 2 Pros: SQL Performance Tuning Techniques Using Wait Statistics, Types & Queues ISBN: 1-4662-3477-6.

What is FILLFACTOR?

The FILLFACTOR setting was introduced in SQL Server 2000 and helps prevent the need for pages to split. We can tell SQL Server not to fill up every section of every page on the first sweep of data. We can instruct it to leave some empty space for later inserts, so we don't have to move around the other existing pieces of data. For a lesson on FILLFACTOR see Chapter 8 of SQL Architecture Basics Joes 2 Pros Volume 3 ISBN: 1451579462.

A FILLFACTOR is one of the important arguments that can be used while creating an index. According to MSDN, FILLFACTOR specifies a percentage that indicates how much the database engine should fill each index page during index creation or rebuild. The FILLFACTOR is always an integer valued from 1 to 100. The FILLFACTOR option is designed for improving index performance and data storage. By setting the fillfactor value, you specify the percentage of space on each page to be filled with data, reserving free space on each page for future table growth.

Specifying a fillfactor value of 70 would imply that 30 percent of each page will be left empty, providing space for index expansion as data is added to the underlying table. The empty space is reserved between the indexed rows rather than at the end of the index. The FILLFACTOR setting applies only when the index is created or rebuilt. (Read more here http://bit.ly/sqlinterview112)

What are points to remember while using the FILLFACTOR argument?

1. If the FILLFACTOR is set to 100 or 0, the database engine fills pages to their capacity while creating indexes.
2. The server-wide default FILLFACTOR is set to 0.
3. To modify the server-wide default value, use the sp_configure system stored procedure.
4. To view the FILLFACTOR value of one or more indexes, use sys.indexes.
5. To modify or set the FILLFACTOR value for individual indexes, use CREATE INDEX or ALTER INDEX statements.
6. Creating a clustered index with a FILLFACTOR < 100 may significantly increase the amount of space the data occupies because the database engine physically reallocates the data while building the clustered index. (Read more here http://bit.ly/sqlinterview113)

Pinal Dave / Vinod Kumar
SQLAuthority.com /ExtremeExperts.com

What is the comparison of SQL Server '100' and '0' FILLFACTOR values?

FILLFACTOR settings of 0 and 100 are equal! (Read more here http://bit.ly/sqlinterview114)

What is PAD_INDEX?

PAD_INDEX is the percentage of free space applied to the intermediate-level pages of the index as specified by the FILLFACTOR. The PAD_INDEX option is useful only when the FILLFACTOR is specified.

What is the difference between a view and a materialized view?

A *view* takes the output of a query and makes it appear like a virtual table. A view can be used in place of tables. A *materialized view* provides indirect access to table data by storing the results of a query in a separate schema object. To create a materialized view you need to put an index on the view.

What is the concept 'optimize for ad hoc workloads' option?

In SQL Server 2008, the "optimize for ad hoc workloads" option is a new server configuration option used to improve the efficiency of the plan cache for workloads that contain many single use ad hoc batches. This option is greatly useful for third party applications that the DBA might not have control over – ERP, CRM systems are typical here.

Pinal Dave / Vinod Kumar
SQLAuthority.com /ExtremeExperts.com

When this option is set to 1, the database engine stores a small compiled plan stub instead of the full compiled plan. This plan stub is created when a batch is compiled for the first time. This helps to relieve memory pressure by not allowing the plan cache to become filled with compiled plans that are not reused.

Setting **optimize for ad hoc workloads** to 1 affects only new plans; plans that are already in the plan cache are unaffected.

What is policy management?

Policy management in SQL SERVER 2008 allows you to define and enforce policies for configuring and managing SQL Server across the enterprise. Policy-based management is configured in SQL Server Management Studio (SSMS). Navigate to the Object Explorer and expand the *management* node and under that is the *policy management* node. In policy management you will see the *policies, conditions,* and *facets* nodes. (Read more here http://bit.ly/sqlinterview115)

What are the basics of policy management?

SQL server 2008 has introduced a policy management framework, which is the latest technique for the SQL server database engine. The SQL policy administrator uses SQL Server Management Studio to create policies that can handle entities on the server side like SQL Server objects and the instance of SQL Server databases.

The policy management framework consists of three components: policy administrators (who create policies), policy management, and explicit administration. Policy-based management in SQL Server assists the database administrators in defining and enforcing policies that tie to database objects and instances. These policies allow the administrator to configure and manage SQL Server across the enterprise. (Read more here http://bit.ly/sqlinterview116)

What are the policy management terms?

To have a better grip on the concept of policy-based management, there are some key terms you need to understand:

Target – A type of entity that is appropriately managed by policy-based management. A target can be a table, database or index, to name a few.

Facet - A property that can be managed in policy-based management. A clear example of a facet is the name of a trigger or the auto shrink property of database.

Conditions – Criteria that specify the state of a facet to true or false. For example, you can adjust the state of a facet that gives you clear specifications of all stored procedures in the schema named 'Banking'.

Policy – A set of rules specified for the server objects or the properties of database.

(Read more here http://bit.ly/sqlinterview117)

What are the advantages of policy management?

The following advantages can be achieved by appropriate administration of policy management system:

- It interacts with various policies for successful system configuration.

Pinal Dave / Vinod Kumar
SQLAuthority.com /ExtremeExperts.com

- It handles the changes in the systems that are the result of configurations against authoring policies.
- It reduces the cost of ownership with a simple elaboration of administration tasks.
- It detects various compliance issues in SQL Server Management Studio.

(Read more here http://bit.ly/sqlinterview118)

What is transparent data encryption?

Transparent data encryption (TDE) introduces a new database option that encrypts the database files automatically, without needing to alter any applications. This prevents unauthorized users from accessing a database, even if they obtain the database files or database backup files.

Transparent data encryption (TDE) performs real-time I/O encryption and decryption of the data and log files. The encryption uses a database encryption key (DEK), which is stored in the database boot record for availability during recovery.

When enabling TDE, you should immediately back up the certificate and the private key associated with the certificate.

What is "Extensible Key Management" in SQL Server?

The Extensible Key Management (EKM) feature allows third-party enterprise key management and Hardware Security Module (HSM) vendors to register their devices in SQL Server. Once registered, SQL Server users can use the encryption keys stored on these modules, as well as leveraging the advanced encryption features that these modules support. Examples include bulk encryption/decryption and many key management functions such as key aging and key rotation. Data can be encrypted and decrypted using TSQL cryptographic statements, and SQL Server uses the external EKM device as the key store.

> By default, Extensible Key Management is off. To enable this feature, use the sp_configure command.

What are signed modules?

SQL Server 2005 introduced the capability to sign modules within the database, such as stored procedures, functions, triggers and assemblies. The need to encrypt the definition or the logic inside these procedures and functions has been there for a long time in enterprises. Signed modules are an efficient and powerful way to do the same for SQL Server. By signing a module with a certificate, the certificate is then granted the relevant permission and goes beyond what can be achieved with the *Execute As* feature, especially from an auditing perspective.

> Data Definition Language (DDL) triggers cannot be signed.

How do we use DBCC commands?

The Transact-SQL programming language provides DBCC statements that act as Database Consistency Commands for SQL Server. DBCC commands are used to perform the following tasks:

- Maintenance tasks on a database, index, or filegroup.
- Tasks that gather and display various types of information.
- Validation operations on a database, table, index, catalog, filegroup, or allocation of database pages.
- Miscellaneous tasks such as enabling trace flags or removing a DLL from memory. (Read more here http://bit.ly/sqlinterview119)

What is the difference between ROLLBACK IMMEDIATE and WITH NO_WAIT during ALTER DATABASE?

ROLLBACK AFTER integer [SECONDS] | ROLLBACK IMMEDIATE:
Specifies whether to roll back after a specified number of seconds or immediately if the transaction is not complete.
NO_WAIT:
Specifies that if the requested database state or option change cannot complete immediately without waiting for transactions to commit or roll back on their own, then the database state or option change request will fail. (Read more here http://bit.ly/sqlinterview120)

What is database mirroring?

Database mirroring involves two copies of a single database that typically reside on different computers. At any given time, only one copy of the database is currently available to clients, which is known as the principal database. Updates made by the clients to the principal database are applied to the other

Pinal Dave / Vinod Kumar SQLAuthority.com /ExtremeExperts.com copy of the database, known as the mirror database. Mirroring involves applying the transaction log from every insertion, update, or delete made on the principal database to the mirror database.

What are the Database Mirroring (DBM) Enhancements done with SQL Server 2008 R2?

There were a number of enhancements done with DBM, some to call out are:

- Write-ahead on the incoming log stream on the mirror server.
- Improved use of "Log Send" buffers.
- Compression of the stream of transaction log records.
- Automatic Recovery from Corrupted Pages.

What is peer-to-peer replication?

Peer-to-peer replication is a special type of transactional replication extension which provides a scale-out and high-availability solution by maintaining copies of data across multiple server instances. Peer-to-peer replication propagates transactionally consistent changes in near real-time. To avoid potential data inconsistency, make sure that you avoid conflicts in a peer-to-peer topology, even with conflict detection enabled.

Conflict detection on peer-to-peer replication was introduced with SQL Server 2008 R2.

Pinal Dave / Vinod Kumar
SQLAuthority.com /ExtremeExperts.com

What is bidirectional transactional replication?

Bidirectional transactional replication is a specific form of transactional replication that allows both the publisher and the subscriber to send data to each other. This is not often used since a better option here would be to use peer-to-peer replication.

What is failover clustering?

With failover clustering, the nodes share disks, but only a single node has access to the database at a time. It is possible to install additional SQL Server failover cluster instances across the nodes; however, this configuration cannot be used to redirect workloads for a single database (for example, separating reads from writes). (Read more here http://bit.ly/sqlinterview121)

What are the questions and considerations you will make for HA/DR design?

- Understand prioritized HA (High Availability) / DR (Disaster Recovery) requirements for the application.
- Are customers comfortable or budgeted for a shared storage solution?
- What is the Recovery Point Objective (RPO)? This decides the combination of configurations like failover clustering. Failover clustering is often deployed alongside database mirroring, with clustering used for local HA, and database mirroring used for DR.
- Consider a geocluster (or stretch cluster) as a combined HA/DR solution. This solution requires

163
Pinal Dave / Vinod Kumar
SQLAuthority.com /ExtremeExperts.com

software to enable the cluster and storage-level replication from the storage vendor.

- What is the Recovery Time Objective (RTO)? This is how fast the system has to get back online after a site failure.

Though these are some of the high level questions, they do help narrow down a solution quickly or at least lead to more solution options.

What is the concept of *Piecemeal Restore* on SQL Server?

Online *Piecemeal Restore* is available from SQL Server 2005 Enterprise Edition onward. This allows administrators of databases that employ multiple filegroups to restore missing filegroups in stages while the database is online.

Piecemeal Restore works with simple, bulk-logged, and full recovery models.

What are OFFLINE datafiles In SQL Server?

The OFFLINE directive is a new feature of the ALTER DATABASE command. This allows databases that employ multiple filegroups to be online serving queries, while some of the database data may be unavailable because one or more filegroup(s) are marked as offline.

Why can't I run TRUNCATE TABLE on a published table?

TRUNCATE TABLE is a minimally-logged operation and it does not fire any triggers. It is not possible to use them on replicated databases because replication cannot track the

Pinal Dave / Vinod Kumar

changes caused by the operation. Transactional replication tracks changes through the transaction log; Merge replication tracks changes through triggers on published tables.

If a stored procedure is encrypted, then can we see its definition in Activity Monitor?

No, we can't see the definition of encrypted stored procedures in Activity Monitor. (Read more here http://bit.ly/sqlinterview122)

SQL Server 2005 introduces "Signed Modules" which is highly recommended for encrypting SPs and functions.

What are the different states a database can get into?

The standard states defined in sys.databases are:

0 = ONLINE

1 = RESTORING

2 = RECOVERING

3 = RECOVERY_PENDING

4 = SUSPECT

5 = EMERGENCY

6 = OFFLINE

How do you stop a log file from growing too big?

If your transaction log file was growing too big and you need to manage its size, then instead of truncating the transaction log file you should choose one of the options mentioned below:

1) **Convert the recovery model to simple recovery:**

   If you change your recovery model to the simple recovery model, then you will not encounter the extraordinary growth of your log file.

2) **Start taking transaction log backup:**

   In the full recovery model, your transaction log will grow until you take a backup of it. You need to take the T-log backup at regular intervals. This way, your log would not grow beyond the size of your interval activity. (Read more here http://bit.ly/sqlinterview123)

What is the Resource Governor in SQL Server?

The Resource Governor is a feature given by SQL Server 2008 to control and allocate CPU and memory resources depending on the priority of applications. The Resource Governor will control the allocation of CPU and memory for the SQL Server Relational Engine Instance.

How would you define the Resource Governor?

The three core fundamental concepts required to define a Resource Governor are:

- **Resource pools** – These define the various groups of resources that can be used within the server. You can define groups for CPU and memory buckets into what workloads are defined.

- **Workload groups** - A workload group serves as a container for session requests so that there can be a predictable performance guaranteed for the group. Typical classifications can be the *CxO group*,

Pinal Dave / Vinod Kumar
SQLAuthority.com /ExtremeExperts.com

the *reporting group*, the *developer group*, and the *admin group* etc.

- **Classification function** – this is based on a set of user-defined criteria contained in a user defined function. The results of the function logic enable the Resource Governor to classify sessions into existing workload groups.

The Resource Governor does not impose any controls on a Dedicated Administrator Connection (DAC).

How do you restart SQL Server in single user mode?

There are a couple of ways to start SQL Server in single user mode:

- Using "SQL Server configuration Manager" (SSCM). Right Click on SQL Server (<Instance Name>) in SSCM, go to properties, advanced tab, append ;-m at the end of existing "startup parameters".
- Using command prompt. Run "net start MSSQLServer /m" command (for default instance) or "net start MSSQL$<InstanceName> /m" (for named instance)
- You can also start sqlservr.exe with –m option from command prompt. To do this, open command prompt, go to the path where you have sqlserver.exe is located and run "sqlservr.exe –m" (for default instance) or sqlservr.exe -m -s<InstanceName> (for named instance)

Pinal Dave / Vinod Kumar
SQLAuthority.com /ExtremeExperts.com

The CHECKPOINT process is not executed when you start an instance of SQL Server in single user mode.

What are the different backup options within SQL Server?

At a high-level the 3 most important backups to understand are:

- **Full backup** – These backups contain ALL the data in a specific database.
- **Differential backup** - A differential backup contains only the data that has changed since the last full database backup. At restore time, the full backup is restored first, followed by the most recent differential backup.
- **Transactional log backups** - The transaction log is a serial record of all the transactions that have been performed against the database since the transaction log was last backed up. With transaction log backups, you can always recover the database to a specific point in time or to the point of failure in a FULL recovery model. You can also recover to a point in time using the bulk logged recovery model if the point in time you want to restore to was not during a bulk insert.

Before you can create the first log backup, you must create a full database backup.

There are other special types of backups which we didn't cover including:

- Partial Backup
- File Backup
- Differential Partial Backup
- Differential File Backup
- Copy-Only Backups

What are the different recovery models inside SQL Server?

There are 3 different recovery models inside SQL Server:

- **Simple recovery model** – This uses minimum administrative overhead for the transaction log, the simple recovery model risks significant work-loss exposure if the database is damaged. Data is recoverable only to the most recent backup. In simple recovery all transactions are truncating the log on each checkpoint.

- **Bulk-logged recovery model** – Used for logging transactions while not filling up the log during bulk operations. This is used for large-scale operations such as bulk import or index creation. Switching temporarily to the bulk-logged recovery model increases performance and reduces log space consumption. Log backups are still required if you want to be able to restore up to the point of failure.

- **Full recovery model** - The full recovery model guarantees the least risk of losing your work if a data file gets damaged. In this model, SQL Server

Pinal Dave / Vinod Kumar
SQLAuthority.com /ExtremeExperts.com

fully logs all operations. In this recovery model, you can recover to any Point-in-time and it is the most recommended model for financial systems.

What is the difference between DB mirroring and log shipping?

Log shipping is one of the oldest forms of high-availability strategies inside SQL Server. The concept here is the primary database on the server is backed up and restored on one or more secondary servers. After this step, transaction logs are restored from the primary database to the secondary database over a periodic interval defined.

Database mirroring provides a redundant copy of a single database that is automatically configured to update the changes. Database mirroring works by sending transaction log records from the main principal database to the mirror server. The transaction log records are then replayed on the mirror database continuously. Some of the differences include:

- A log shipping secondary can also be set to allow read-only access to the database in between transaction log restore operations.
- The log shipping process is controlled through SQL Server agent jobs that perform the backups, copies, restores, and monitoring.
- Database mirroring can detect failures automatically. Even automatic page repairs are possible.
- With database mirroring failovers can also be automated.

Pinal Dave / Vinod Kumar
SQLAuthority.com /ExtremeExperts.com

What are plan guides?

Starting in SQL Server 2005, there is a new feature called Plan Guides that can help out in cases where you discover poorly performing queries that you don't have direct control over (like ones made by third party applications). Plan guides influence optimization of queries by attaching query hints to them. When the query executes, SQL Server matches the query to the plan guide and attaches the OPTION clause to the query at run time.

Plan guides that misuse query hints can cause complications, poor execution, and performance problems.

How can you validate a backup copy of your database?

The best option to validate a backup copy is the RESTORE VERIFYONLY command. This option checks to see that the backup set is complete and the entire backup is readable. However, RESTORE VERIFYONLY does not attempt to verify the structure of the data contained in the backup volumes.

You can also restore a backup to check the validity of a backup copy.

What is the ONLINE rebuilding of index?

An online operation means that when online operations are occurring in the database, then the database is in a normal operational condition. The processes which are participating in online operations do not require exclusive access to the database. In the case of online indexing operations, when index operations (create, rebuild, dropping) occur they do not require exclusive access to the index and do not lock any database tables. This is a major important upgrade in SQL Server from previous versions. (Read more here http://bit.ly/sqlinterview124)

The Online Indexing feature is available only in the Enterprise Edition of SQL Server

What are the basics of table partitioning with SQL Server?

The concept of partitioning is not new to SQL Server. In fact, some form of partitioning has been possible in every release of the product. However, partitioning has traditionally been cumbersome and thus underutilized by DBAs as a strategy. Because of the significant performance gains inherent in the concept, SQL Server 7.0 began improving the feature by enabling forms of partitioning through partitioned views (but not tables). For a lesson on Partitioned Tables see Chapters 8-11 of SQL Architecture Basics Joes 2 Pros Volume 3 ISBN: 1451579462.

While the improvements in SQL Server 7.0 and SQL Server 2000 significantly enhanced performance when using partitioned views, they did not simplify the administration, design, or development of a partitioned dataset. When using partitioned views, all of the base tables (on which the view is defined) must be created and managed individually.

With SQL Server 2005 came a much more accessible and workable process, and SQL Server 2008 now offers the most advanced method for partitioning large datasets through partitioned table. However, the nature of partitioning a table is slightly different from slicing an apple into sections which are then permanently separated. After you partition a table, it remains a single, unified object with its underlying data contained in separate filegroups. This allows the table to function logically as a single object, while its data is physically stored in separate locations.

You can partition a logical set of data into multiple physical storage locations for manageability and performance. Partitions were introduced in SQL Server 2005. Both SQL Server 2005 and SQL Server 2008 allow up to 1000 partitions. Partition functions define boundaries for your tables. One partition function boundary value means two table partitions. The filegroups are the physical locations for these partitions. The main reason for partitioning a table is to get improved performance when executing DML on a large table.

A partition scheme maps the partitions to the filegroups. The partition scheme is used to create a partitioned table. The partition function sets datatype and range values. The partition scheme maps the partitions to the filegroups.

To create partition tables do your steps in this order:
1. Create the files and filegroups.
2. Create the partition function.
3. Create the partition scheme.
4. Create the table.
5. Populate the table.

What are the steps to create a table partition?

If you already have your files and filegroups set up, what are the 3 steps for creating a table partition:

- Partition function – This defines *how* you want to partition the data.
- Partition scheme – This defines *where* each of the partitions defined by the function will reside.
- Attaching the partition scheme to a table – You map the partition scheme to the table based on a column's data using the ON clause in table definition.

Below is a code sample of how to create a partition function, use that function in a partition scheme and then base a partitioned table on the partition scheme:

```
CREATE PARTITION FUNCTION
pf_OrderDate(Datetime)
AS RANGE RIGHT
FOR VALUES
('1/1/2007','1/1/2008','1/1/2009','1/1/2010')

CREATE PARTITION SCHEME ps_OrderDate
AS PARTITION pf_OrderDate
TO (fg2006, fg2007, fg2008, fg2009, fg2010)

CREATE TABLE dbo.SalesInvoiceHorizontal
(     [InvoiceID] [int] NOT NULL,
      [OrderDate] [datetime] NOT NULL,
      [PaidDate] [datetime] NOT NULL,
      [CustomerID] [int] NOT NULL,
      [Comment] [ntext] NULL, )
ON ps_OrderDate(OrderDate)
```

Pinal Dave / Vinod Kumar
SQLAuthority.com /ExtremeExperts.com

SQL Server 2008 R2 Data Center Edition supports up to 15000 partitions.

What are the various page verification options in SQL Server 2008?

Between the time SQL Server writes a page to disk, and then later reads the same page, it is possible that the data stored in the page may get corrupted due to circumstances outside the control of SQL Server. While SQL Server cannot prevent corruption outside of its control, it does at least have the ability to identify corrupt data. In SQL Server 2005 and SQL Server 2008, you can choose from one of three PAGE_VERIFY options:

- NONE
- CHECKSUM
- TORN_PAGE_DETECTION

CHECKSUM works by calculating a checksum over the contents of the whole page and stores the value in the page header when a page is written to disk. When the page is read from disk, the CHECKSUM is recomputed and compared to the CHECKSUM value stored in the page header. A CHECKSUM failure indicates an I/O path problem.

We highly recommend using CHECKSUM for all new databases.

What are some of the operations that cannot be done in the model database?

Some of the restrictions when working with the model database are as follows:

- We cannot add files or filegroups.
- The default collation is the server collation and cannot be changed.
- We cannot drop this database.
- Setting the database to OFFLINE is not available.
- Setting the database or primary filegroup to READ_ONLY mode is not allowed.

How can Index fragmentation be removed inside SQL Server?

Some of the most common methods of removing fragmentation use the following DDL statements:

- CREATE INDEX...DROP EXISTING
- ALTER INDEX...REORGANIZE
- ALTER INDEX...REBUILD
- DROP INDEX *and then* CREATE INDEX

For a lesson on Index Fragmentation see Chapter 11 of SQL Architecture Basics Joes 2 Pros Volume 3 ISBN: 1451579462.

How can you disable indices inside SQL Server?

As an administrator, disabling indexes is a feature which is available in SQL Server 2005 and later versions to prevent the index usage by user queries. When you are disabling an index the index definition remains in metadata and index statistics

Pinal Dave / Vinod Kumar
SQLAuthority.com /ExtremeExperts.com

are also kept for non-clustered indexes. You can use the following command to disable an index:

```
ALTER INDEX IX_Address_StateProvinceID ON
Person.Address DISABLE
```

To re-enable an index you might think the syntax would be to use the ENABLE keyword. In fact the following command can be used or CREATE INDEX WITH DROP_EXISTING Statement can be used –

```
ALTER INDEX IX_Address_StateProvinceID ON
Person.Address REBUILD
```

Pinal Dave / Vinod Kumar
SQLAuthority.com /ExtremeExperts.com

Data Warehousing Interview Questions & Answers

An expert is someone called in at the last minute to share the blame. - Sam Ewing.

What is Business Intelligence (BI)?

Business Intelligence (BI) refers to technologies, applications and practices for the collection, integration, analysis, and presentation of business information and sometimes to the information itself. The purpose of BI is to support better business decision making. Thus, BI is also described as a Decision Support System (DSS).

BI systems provide historical, current, and predictive views of business operations, most often using data that has been gathered into a data warehouse or a data mart and occasionally working from operational data.

What is data warehousing?

A data warehouse is the main repository of an organization's historical data (its corporate memory). It contains the raw material for management's Decision Support System (DSS). The critical factor leading to the use of a data warehouse is

Pinal Dave / Vinod Kumar
SQLAuthority.com /ExtremeExperts.com

that a data analyst can perform complex queries and analysis, such as data mining, on the information without slowing down the operational systems (Ref: Wikipedia). A data warehousing collection of data is designed to support management decision making. Data warehouses contain a wide variety of data that present a coherent picture of business conditions at a single point in time. It is a repository of integrated information, available for queries and analysis.

What are some characteristics of typical data warehousing?

- **Subject-oriented**: Means that the data in the database is organized so that all of the data elements relating to the same real-world event or object are linked together.

- **Time-variant**: Means that the changes to the data in the database are tracked and recorded so that reports can be produced showing changes over time.

- **Non-volatile:** Means that data in the database is never over-written or deleted, once committed, the data is static, read-only, but retained for future reporting.

- **Integrated**: Means that the database contains data from most or all of an organization's operational applications, and that this data is made consistent.

What languages are used for BI workloads?

BI uses the following languages for achieving business goals.

MDX – Multidimensional Expressions:

This language is mainly used for retrieving data from SSAS cubes. It looks very similar to T-SQL, but it is very different in the areas of conceptualization and implementation.

DMX – Data Mining Extensions:

DMX deals with data mining structures. This is also used for SQL Server Analysis Services (SSAS), but rather than cubes it is used for data mining structures. This language is more complicated than MDX. Microsoft has provided many wizards in its BI tools, which further reduced the number of available experts for learning this language.

XMLA – XML for analysis:

This is mainly used for SSAS administrative tasks. It is quite commonly used in administration tasks such as backing up or restoring databases, copying and moving databases, or for learning metadata information. Again, Microsoft BI tools provide a lot of wizards for these administrative tasks. (Read more here http://bit.ly/sqlinterview125)

DAX – Data Analysis Expressions:

The Data Analysis Expressions (DAX) language is a new formula language that you can use in *PowerPivot* workbooks. DAX is not a subset of MDX, but a new formula language that is considered an extension of the formula language in Excel.

Pinal Dave / Vinod Kumar
SQLAuthority.com /ExtremeExperts.com

DAX is not a query language; it is an expression language supported only within PowerPivot for Excel.

What is a dimension table?

A dimension table contains textual attributes of measurements stored in the facts tables. A dimensional table is a collection of hierarchies, categories, and logic which can be used for a user to traverse in hierarchical nodes.

What is a hierarchy?

A hierarchy is the specification of levels that represent relationships between different attributes within a dimension. For example, one possible hierarchy in the Time dimension is Year → Quarter → Month → Day.

What is a fact table?

To be clear, people can get business measurements and fact measurements confused. It would be a *fact* measurement to say that I bought a cup of coffee at Starbucks yesterday. A business measurement might be that sales for Starbucks are up 8% over last year.

Fact tables contain measurements of individual business processes. Fact tables contain the foreign keys for linking to dimension tables. For instance, if your business process is *paper production* you might need to know the product each day for each machine in each of your factories. That is a lot of granular data. From this you could write an aggregated query or build a cube to find out business measurements like

Pinal Dave / Vinod Kumar
SQLAuthority.com /ExtremeExperts.com

"average production of paper by one machine" or "weekly production of paper from all machines". That will be considered as the measurement of business process which came from many rows (or facts) in the fact table.

As a best practice - do not update fact tables - only add new rows. The warehouse reflects the "truth" at the time you knew it.

What does the level of granularity of a fact table mean?

Level of granularity means the level of detail put into fact tables in a data warehouse. Level of granularity implies the detail you are willing to use for each transactional fact.

What is a conformed fact?

Conformed dimensions are the dimensions which can be used across multiple data marts in combination with multiple fact tables accordingly.

What are non-additive facts?

Non-additive facts are facts that cannot be summed up for any of the dimensions present in the fact table. A good example of this is measuring your product Inventory. If your inventory last week was 10 and this week was 12, then the sum of 22 for the month makes no sense. Inventory is considered a non-additive measure to the Inventory field in the fact table and would thus be a non-additive fact. However, Inventory is not considered to be a useless measure but is critical to your business. If there are changes in dimensions (not the time dimension), then the same facts can be useful.

What are aggregate tables?

Aggregate tables are used to store summaries of fact tables. These are typically methods used to improve performance and can also be used with OLTP workloads. OLAP cubes contain pre-aggregated tables based on their modeling.

What is dimensional modeling?

The Dimensional Data Model concept involves two types of tables and it is different from the 3rd normal form. This concept uses *Facts* tables, which contain the measurements of the business, and d*imension* tables, which contain the context (dimension of calculation) of the measurements.

What are conformed dimensions?

Conformed dimensions mean the exact same thing with every possible fact table to which they are joined. They are common to the cubes.

What are Slowly Changing Dimensions (SCD)?

SCD is the abbreviation for Slowly Changing Dimension. SCD applies to cases where the attribute for a record varies over time. There are three different types of SCD:

1) SCD1: The new record replaces the original record. Only one record exists in database - current data.

2) SCD2: A new record is added into the customer dimension table. Two records exist in the database - current data and previous history data.

3) SCD3: The original data is modified to include new data. One record exists in the database - new

information is attached with old information in the same row.

What is a hybrid Slowly Changing Dimension?

Hybrid SCDs are a combination of both SCD 1 and SCD 2. It may happen that in a table, some columns are important and we need to track changes for them, i.e. capture the historical data for them, whereas in some columns even if the data changes, we do not care.

How do you load the time dimension?

Time dimensions are usually loaded by a program that loops through all possible dates that may appear in the data. 100 years may be represented in a time dimension, with one row per day.

Why is data modeling important?

Data modeling is probably the most labor intensive and time consuming part of the development process. The goal of the data model is to make sure that all the data objects required by the database are completely and accurately represented. Because the data model uses easily understood notations and natural language, it can be reviewed and verified as correct by the end users.

In computer science, data modeling is the process of creating a data model by applying a data model theory to create a data model instance. A data model theory is a formal data model description. In data modeling, we are structuring and organizing data. These data structures are then typically

Pinal Dave / Vinod Kumar

implemented in a database management system. In addition to defining and organizing the data, data modeling will impose (implicitly or explicitly) constraints or limitations on the data placed within the structure.

Managing large quantities of structured and unstructured data is a primary function of information systems. Data models describe structured data for storage in data management systems such as relational databases. They typically do not describe unstructured data, such as word processing documents, email messages, pictures, digital audio, and video. (Reference: Wikipedia)

What are the fundamental stages of data warehousing?

There are four different stages of the data warehousing lifecycle: Offline Operational Databases, Offline Data Warehouse, Real Time Data Warehouse, and Integrated Data Warehouse.

Offline operational databases:

Data warehouses in this initial stage are developed by simply copying the database of an operational system to an off-line server where the processing load of reporting does not have an impact on the operational system's performance.

Offline data warehouse:

Data warehouses in this stage of evolution are updated on a regular time cycle (usually daily, weekly or monthly) from the operational systems, and the data is stored in an integrated reporting-oriented data structure.

Real time data warehouse:

Data warehouses at this stage are updated on a transaction or event basis, every time an operational system performs a transaction (e.g. an order or a delivery or a booking).

Integrated data warehouse:

Data warehouses at this stage are used to generate activity or transactions that are passed back into the operational systems for use in the daily activity of the organization. (Reference: Wikipedia)

What are the different methods of loading dimension tables?

There are two different ways to load data in dimension tables, *conventional* and *direct*.

Conventional (Slow):

All the constraints and keys are validated against the data before it is loaded; this way data integrity is maintained at all times.

Direct (Fast):

All the constraints and keys are disabled before the data is loaded. Once data is loaded, it is validated against all of the constraints and keys. If data is found to be invalid, it is not included in its index and all future processes on this data are skipped.

Describe the foreign key columns in fact tables and dimension tables.

Foreign keys of dimension tables are primary keys of fact tables (entity tables). Foreign keys of facts tables are primary keys of dimension tables.

What is data mining?

Data mining is the process of analyzing data from different perspectives and summarizing it into useful information. Data mining takes the analysis to the next stage by applying models on test data to get trends, hidden correlations of attributes, and even build probability scenarios for future data.

What is the difference between OLTP and OLAP?

Data source
OLTP: Operational data is from the original data source
OLAP: Consolidation data is from various sources.

Process goal
OLTP: A snapshot of business processes which do the fundamental business tasks for the group or organization.
OLAP: Multi-dimensional views of business activities of planning and decision making.

Queries and process scripts
OLTP: Simple quick running queries run by the users.
OLAP: Complex long running queries by the system to update the aggregated data.

Database design

OLTP: A Normalized small database. Speed will be not an issue because it is a small database, and normalization will not degrade performance. This adopts the entity relationship (ER) model and an application-oriented database design.

OLAP: A De-normalized large database. Speed is an issue because of a large database using de-normalization will improve performance as there will be fewer tables to scan while performing tasks. This adopts a star, snowflake or fact constellation mode of subject-oriented database design.

Back up and system administration

OLTP: A regular database backup and system administration can take care of all your backup and restore needs.

OLAP: Reloading data from the OLTP data back into OLAP is considered as a good backup option for OLAP.

What is the difference between OLAP and a data warehouse?

A data warehouse is the place where the data is stored for analysis, whereas OLAP is the process of analyzing the data, managing aggregations, partitioning information into cubes for in depth visualization. OLAP is the process that consumes your data warehouse.

What is ODS?

ODS is the abbreviation of Operational Data Store. This is a database structure that is a repository for near real-time operational data rather than long-term trend data. The ODS may further become the enterprise-shared operational database, allowing operational systems that are being re-engineered to use the ODS as their operation databases.

What is ETL?

ETL is abbreviation of Extract, Transform, and Load. ETL is a software process that enables businesses to consolidate their disparate data into one catalog. While moving data from place to place, it doesn't really matter that the data is in different forms or formats. The data can come from any source.

ETL is powerful enough to handle such data disparities. First, the extract function reads data from a specified source database and extracts a desired subset of data. Next, the transform function works with the acquired data - using rules or lookup tables, or creating combinations with other data - to convert it to the desired state. Finally, the load function is used to write the resulting data to a target database.

What is VLDB?

VLDB is the abbreviation for Very Large Database. For instance, a one-terabyte database can be considered as a VLDB. Typically, these are decision support systems or transaction processing applications serving a large number of users.

Is OLTP a database designed optimally for a data warehouse?

No. OLTP database tables are normalized, and it will add additional time to queries to return results. Additionally, the OLTP database is small; it does not contain data from a long

Pinal Dave / Vinod Kumar
SQLAuthority.com /ExtremeExperts.com

period (many years), which needs to be analyzed. An OLTP system is basically an ER model and not a dimensional model. If a complex query is executed on an OLTP system, it may lead to heavy overhead on the OLTP server that will affect the normal business processes.

If denormalizing improves data warehouse processes, then why is the fact table in normal form?

The foreign keys of facts tables are primary keys of dimension tables. It is clear that the fact table contains columns which are a primary key to another table that in itself makes it a normal form table.

What are lookup tables?

A lookup table is the table placed on the target table based upon the primary key of the target. It just updates the table by allowing only modified (new or updated) records based on the lookup condition.

What is real-time data-warehousing?

Data warehousing captures business activity data. Real-time data warehousing captures business activity data as it occurs. As soon as the business activity is complete and there is data for it, the completed activity data flows into the data warehouse and becomes available instantly.

What is a BUS schema?

A BUS schema consists of a master suite of confirmed dimensions and standardized definitions of facts.

What is a star schema?

A star schema is a way of organizing the tables such that we can retrieve the result from the database quickly in the warehouse environment.

What is a snowflake schema?

In a snowflake schema, each dimension has a primary dimension table, to which one or more additional dimensions can join. The primary dimension table is the only table that can join to the fact table.

What are the differences between the star and snowflake schemas?

Star schema: A single fact table with N number of dimensions; all dimensions will be linked directly with a fact table. This schema is de-normalized and results in a simple join and less complex queries as well as faster results.

Snowflake schema: Any dimension with extended dimensions is known as a snowflake schema; dimensions maybe interlinked or may have one-to-many relationships with other tables. This schema is normalized, and results in complex joins needing very complex queries (as well as slower results).

What is an ER diagram?

Entity Relationship (ER) diagrams are a major data modeling tool and will help organize the data in your project into entities and define the relationships between the entities. This process has enabled the analyst to produce a good database

Pinal Dave / Vinod Kumar
SQLAuthority.com /ExtremeExperts.com

structure so that the data can be stored and retrieved in a most efficient manner.

An Entity Relationship (ER) diagram is a specialized graphic that illustrates the interrelationships between entities in a database. A type of diagram used in data modeling for relational data bases. These diagrams show the structure of each table and the links between tables.

What is the difference between ER modeling and dimensional modeling?

ER modeling is used for normalizing the OLTP database design. Dimensional modeling is used for de-normalizing the OLAP design.

What is a degenerate dimension table?

If a table contains values, which are neither dimensional values nor measures, then it is called a degenerate dimension table.

What is a surrogate key?

A surrogate key is a substitution for the natural primary key. Surrogated keys are always integer or numeric. It is just a unique identifier or number for each row that can be used for the primary key to the table. The only requirement for a surrogate primary key is that it should be unique for each row in the table. It is useful because the natural primary key can change and this makes updates more difficult.

Pinal Dave / Vinod Kumar
SQLAuthority.com /ExtremeExperts.com

What is a junk dimension?

Any number of very small dimensions may get lumped together to form a single dimension, i.e. a junk dimension - the attributes are not closely related. Grouping of random flags and text attributes in a dimension and moving them to a single separate sub dimension is known as junk dimension.

What is a data mart?

A Data Mart (DM) is a specialized version of a Data Warehouse (DW). Like data warehouses, data marts contain a snapshot of operational data that helps business people to strategize based on analyses of past trends and experiences. The key difference is that the creation of a data mart is predicated on a specific, predefined need for a certain grouping and configuration of select data. A data mart configuration emphasizes easy access to relevant information (Reference: Wiki). Data marts are designed to help the manager make strategic decisions about their business.

What is a cube and linked cube with reference to a data warehouse?

Cubes are logical representations of multidimensional data. The edge of the cube contains dimension members and the body of the cube contains data values. The linking in a cube ensures that the data in the cubes remain consistent.

What is a snapshot with reference to a data warehouse?

You can disconnect the report from the catalog to which it is attached by saving the report with a snapshot of the data.

What is MDS?

Master Data Services or MDS helps enterprises standardize the data people rely on to make critical business decisions. With Master Data Services, IT organizations can centrally manage critical data assets companywide and across diverse systems. This can enable more people to securely manage master data directly, and ensure the integrity of information over time. (Read more here http://bit.ly/sqlinterview126)

Explain the paradigm of Bill Inmon and Ralph Kimball.

Bill Inmon's paradigm: A data warehouse is one part of the overall business intelligence system. An enterprise has one data warehouse, and data marts source their information from the data warehouse. In the data warehouse, information is stored in the 3rd normal form.

Ralph Kimball's paradigm: A data warehouse is the conglomerate of all data marts within the enterprise. Information is always stored in the dimensional model.

What are the different kinds of report parameters?

Reporting services uses two different kinds of parameters -

Query Parameter:

- The query parameters are defined as part of the dataset query and processed on the database server.
- If the query contains a query parameter, Reporting Services automatically creates a report parameter based on the name of the query parameter. Query parameters are mapped to report parameters so that

users or report authors can pass back the value to use in the query.

Report Parameter:

- A report parameter is a variable defined at the report level that allows the personalization of a reports at run time.

- Report parameters differ from query parameters in that they are defined in a report and processed by the report server.

- Each time you add a report parameter to the report, a new member is added to the Parameters Collection for you to use in an expression.

What are the command line tools to execute SSIS packages?

DTSEXECUI – When this command line tool is run a user interface is loaded in order to configure each of the applicable parameters to execute an SSIS package.

DTEXEC – This is a pure command line tool where all of the needed switches must be passed into the command for successful execution of the SSIS package.

What is control flow inside SSIS?

In SQL Server Integration Services (SSIS) a workflow is called a control-flow. A control-flow links together the various data-flows as a series of operations in order to achieve the final result. A control flow consists of one or more tasks and containers that execute when the package runs.

Pinal Dave / Vinod Kumar
SQLAuthority.com /ExtremeExperts.com

What are the different control flow elements inside SSIS?

SSIS provides three different types of control flow elements: containers that provide structures in packages, tasks that provide functionality, and precedence constraints that connect the executables, containers, and tasks into an ordered control flow.

What is a data flow?

A data flow consists of the sources and destinations that extract and load data, the transformations that modify and transform data, and the paths that link sources, transformations, and destinations.

Before you can add a data flow to a package, the package control flow must include a data flow task.

What are the different components of a data flow?

SQL Server Integration Services (SSIS) provides three different types of data flow components: sources, transformations, and destinations:

- Sources extract data from data stores such as tables and views in relational databases as well as from sources like files, and Analysis Services databases.
- Transformations modify, summarize, and clean data.
- Destinations load data into data stores or create in-memory datasets.

Explain the different options for dynamic configurations within SSIS?

There are basically 4 different ways of storing and accessing configuration information from within SSIS:

- Use an XML config file.
- Use custom environmental variables.
- Use a database per environment with the variables.
- Use a centralized database with all variables.

What are the different lookup cache modes in SSIS?

There are basically 3 cache modes available in SSIS Lookup Transformations and are listed as follows:

- Full Cache Mode
- Partial Cache Mode
- No Cache Mode

Explain partial cache mode?

In partial cache mode, SSIS queries the database for new rows coming in from the source and if matched then that row is cached into SSIS lookup cache for rows coming in subsequently in the data flow. When the cache becomes full, SSIS removes a few of the rows from cache based on the usage / match statistics for those rows and loads the new matching rows into the Lookup Cache.

What is the use of the SSIS Data Profiler?

SQL Server 2008 introduced the new feature of the Data Profiler with SSIS. The Data Profiler helps you understand the number of distinct values in each column, distribution of data, Mean (average), and standard deviation, Minimum and

Maximum values of the data values, column length distribution, NULL Ratios, column Patterns etc. This is highly recommended during a performance tuning exercise to know your data sampling.

Data Profiler is a great tool to have. In performance testing you might want to mimic data distribution on the production environment to a similar sized distribution on the test environment for a particular columnar data.

What do you mean by repeating data regions inside SSRS?

The concept of nested data regions to display the same data region multiple times in your report is called repeating data regions. Datasets for both data regions must be the same. If you need to create a report that uses grouping like this (such as in a master-detail page) but with different datasets, use a sub-report.

What are the differences between the SSRS 2005 and SSRS 2008 versions?

Report Server 2008 is a complete architectural rewrite; from the report processing engine and the report renderers to the fact that it no longer depends on IIS to host the report server and report manager. The following areas could have major implications for support:

- Removal of IIS as a dependency
- On-Demand "Pull" model of report processing
- Consolidated renderer code
- New data visualization controls
- New Report Designer

Areas with minimal changes are:

- Report Builder
- SharePoint Integration
- Client Print Control
- Report Manager User interface
- Report Server web method APIs
- Command-line tools

What is PowerPivot?

PowerPivot is comprised of numerous different client and server components that provide customers an end to end solution for creating business intelligence via the familiar interface of Microsoft Excel 2010.

PowerPivot for SharePoint adds server-side applications and features that support PowerPivot data access and management for workbooks that you publish to SharePoint. PowerPivot server components loads the data, processes queries, performs scheduled data refresh, and tracks server and workbook usage in the farm.

What is PowerPivot for Excel?

PowerPivot for Excel allows customers to create PowerPivot IMBI (In-Memory Business Intelligence) databases within the Excel process space. The data is stored in the actual workbook itself. The workbook contains the embedded data that is extracted and processed by the Vertipaq engine which is basically Analysis Services running in process inside of excel. There is no need to connect to a server to work with the data once downloaded.

Pinal Dave / Vinod Kumar
SQLAuthority.com /ExtremeExperts.com

The only thing you need is the Excel Add-in for PowerPivot.

What is master data?

Master data is slowly changing reference data shared across systems. This master data describes the critical *nouns* of the business that typically fall into the following categories: people, things, places, or abstract concepts.

SQL Wait Stats Joes 2 Pros: SQL Performance Tuning
Techniques Using Wait Statistics, Types & Queues
ISBN: 1-4662-3477-6 (Joes2Pros.com)

1. Text files only contain data (no metadata). It's up to you to understand what the data means. XML is self-describing data, as it contains both data and metadata.

2. A wait stat happens when SQL Server wants to execute a task and it has to wait for resources to execute the task.

3. A task can be in one of three states:

    • Suspended

    • Runnable

    • Running

4. The key dynamic management view (DMV) that helps us to understand wait stats is sys.dm_os_wait_stats.

5. To reset the wait stats in sys.dm_os_wait_stats DMV following use the command:

    o DBCC SQLPERF('sys.dm_os_wait_stats', CLEAR)

6. If a session is waiting on a lock, then the blocking_session_id column of the sys.dm_os_waiting_tasks DMV will have the session_id of the lock.

7. The sql_handle of the sys.dm_exec_requests DMV points to the memory space of the actual SQL code being used by the task

8. You can get the SQL code from the sys.dm_exec_sql_text Dynamic Management Function (DMF) by passing in the SQL handle

9. A baseline is a measure of how things were going before you made any changes.

10. Parallel executions are important for computing since it allows more processing power (worker threads) at higher speed to be used for a single task.

11. There is an organizer-coordinator thread (thread 0), which creates organized worker threads into tasks which wait for all the worker threads to complete before the task can be closed.

12. When a big task has multiple threads starting at the same time, they won't always finish at the same time. When one or more of the threads will lag behind, thread 0 has to wait for all threads to finish, thereby creating the CXPACKET wait stat.

13. Note that not all the CXPACKET wait types are bad, since they only exist during parallel execution (i.e., which usually make things run faster).

14. Small tasks should not use multiple worker threads and will run more efficiently with just one thread.

15. Data-warehousing / Reporting servers tend to have very large tasks. They benefit from parallelism and will invariably have some CXPACKET wait types while large projects finish processing.

16. You will have little to no CXPACKET wait time with well-balanced parallelism or simple single CPU serial operation.

17. Mixed systems (OLTP + OLAP) present more of a challenge and the right balance must be found

General Best Practices

Here are some quick notes on some generic best practices. These are sometimes subjective based on the situation but we consider these can still apply to most of the systems we work with. Don't take these words as written in stone but just as guiding content:

- **Do** de-normalize if necessary for performance.
- **Do** define the Primary Key as clustered (unless you are using a Surrogate Key). This keeps the secondary indexes much smaller.
- **Do** create indexes on the Foreign Key columns.
- **Do** select the correct "Recovery Model" for a database.
- **Do** use 100% FILLFACTOR on read-only or seldom updated tables.
- **Do Not** over-index, make sure you know which indexes will be used.
- **Do Not** use special characters when creating database objects.
- **Do** use consistent abbreviations of similar words. If "Charge" is CHRG then "Change" should be something different like CHNG.
- **Do Not** use spaces or special characters in column names.
- iSCSI storage area networks is a viable solution where cost is an issue.
- Use redundant, dedicated gigabit Ethernet NICs for iSCSI connectivity.
- **Do not** enable network protocols unless they are needed.

- **Do not** expose a server that is running SQL Server to the public Internet.
- Make sure the tables have statistics. Keeping Auto Generate Statistics and Auto Create Statistics options on in the database is the default. For read only databases, it may be necessary to manually create statistics.
- **No undocumented** system stored procedures should be used.
- When calling a stored procedure with parameters, it's a good idea to name the parameter and the value instead of just supplying the values in order. In other words pass parameters by name and not position.
- **Avoid** altering the ANSI settings with SET in procedures, as doing so causes stored procedures to recompile.
- Having datatype mismatches between columns that are in a primary/foreign key relationship or for parameters and values that are mismatched must be avoided.
- **Do not** implement security as an afterthought in the development process.
- Use "allow only encrypted connections" only if needed for end-to-end encryption of sensitive sessions.
- Grant CONNECT permission only on endpoints to logins that need to use them. Explicitly deny CONNECT permission to endpoints that are not needed by users or groups.
- Install only those components that you will immediately use. Additional components can always be installed as needed.

Pinal Dave / Vinod Kumar
SQLAuthority.com / ExtremeExperts.com

- **Turn off** unneeded services by setting the service to either Manual startup or Disabled.
- Anti-Virus software installed on the server should be properly configured to exclude the file extensions used by SQL Server (mdf, ndf, ldf, bak, trn, log etc).
- Always stay as current of a version as possible.
- Pre-size your Transaction Log files and Data files and don't set them to auto-grow.
- Separate transaction log files from data and tempdb volumes.
- Size the tempdb database appropriately. For example, if you use the SORT_IN_TEMPDB option when you rebuild indexes, be sure to have sufficient free space in tempdb to store sorting operations.
- Use CHECKSUM on the tempdb and user defined databases.
- Use Wait Stats and Windows System Monitor (perfmon) in conjunction to get an idea of what is really going on within the server.
- Use sys.dm_db_index_physical_stats to determine the amount of index fragmentation.
- Use the AUTO CREATE and AUTO UPDATE of statistics (the system default in SQL Server).
- Plan to use the backup compression feature of SQL Server 2008 Enterprise Edition.
- Backup LUN - Place backups on separate physical spindles. Do not backup to the same location as your database data files.
- Prefer sp_executesql over simply calling Exec @sql.

Pinal Dave / Vinod Kumar
SQLAuthority.com /ExtremeExperts.com

- Prefer "SELECT TOP (1)" versus "SELECT TOP 1". The former is required by ANSI.
- The SQL server services do not need to run under an administrator context or the local system. It is recommended that you create a low privileged windows account that you want the SQL server service to run as.
- Assume that damage is possible and have an aggressive backup policy. Back up all data regularly and store copies in a secure off-site location.
- Ensure that the mapping between database users and logins at the server level are correct. This can be a problem in cases where databases are detached and attached to other servers.
- Use Scope_Identity() rather than @@Identity.

Please send errata, suggestions and feedback to

books@sqlauthority.com

SQLAuthority.com /ExtremeExperts.com
Pinal Dave / Vinod Kumar

Annexure

This book assumes at least an intermediate knowledge of SQL Server. This can be from a combination of experience and training. You need to already have a knowledge of queries, programming objects (like tables and stored procedures), and indexes. If you are new to the field but have done extensive studies, then this book assumes you have been exposed to the concepts in the first four of the five SQL *Joes 2 Pros* SQL development books:

Beginning SQL Joes 2 Pros: The SQL Hands-On Guide for Beginners
ISBN 1-4392-5317-X

SQL Queries Joes 2 Pros: SQL Query Techniques for Microsoft SQL Server 2008
ISBN 1-4392-5318-8

SQL Architecture Basics Joes 2 Pros: Core Architecture Concepts
ISBN: 1-4515-7946-2

SQL Programming Development Joes 2 Pros: Programming & Development for Microsoft SQL Server 2008
ISBN: 1-4515-7948-9

SQL Interoperability Joes 2 Pros: SQL 2008 Techniques with XML, C#, and PowerShell
ISBN: 1-4515-7950-0

SQL Wait Stats Joes 2 Pros: SQL Performance Tuning Techniques Using Wait Statistics, Types & Queues
ISBN: 1-4662-3477-6

Pinal Dave / Vinod Kumar
SQLAuthority.com /ExtremeExperts.com

CPSIA information can be obtained
at www.ICGtesting.com
Printed in the USA
FSOW04n1055160916
25095FS